T0193827

Critical Acclaim for
On the Efficient Determination of Most Near Neighbors
Horseshoes, Hand Grenades, Web Search, and Other Situations When Close is Close Enough

The material in this book grew from a simple question: "We know how to easily determine whether two files are *identical*, but what do we know about determining whether two files are *similar*?" The answer was "Not much," but when a theorist gives this answer, good things often happen. Such was the case here.

This book will be important to practitioners interested in this and similar questions. It contains two intertwined threads; a mathematical treatment of the problem and an engineering thread that provides extremely efficient code for obtaining the solution at scale. I recommend it highly.

Charles P. (Chuck) Thacker
Microsoft Research
2009 Turing Award Winner

From de-duplication to search, billion dollar industries rely on the ability to search for keys that are "close" to a specified key. The book by Mark Manasse provides a beautiful exposition of the field. Manasse is a well-known expert who has written some of the fundamental theoretical papers in the field; better still, he has worked on real products such as AltaVista and Windows file de-duplication. Mark has the rare ability to take theoretical ideas and convert them to sound engineering. The book will appeal to developers working in the web milieu because it illuminates the details that are often missing using code snippets. It will also appeal to researchers and students because of the uniform and insightful exposition of an important area.

George Varghese
Professor
University of California, San Diego

Mark Manasse, the father of micropayments, provides insight, techniques and theory behind search—on getting not too large, not too small, but just right results.

This horseshoes mini-treatise comes right from the horse's mouth as an AltaVista—he shows how the game was constructed by high dimensionality mapping into tractable space and time to find ringers and good outliers.

Gordon Bell
Microsoft Research

On the Efficient Determination of Most Near Neighbors

Horseshoes, Hand Grenades, Web Search, and
Other Situations When Close Is Close Enough

Second Edition

Synthesis Lectures on Information Concepts, Retrieval, and Services

Editor
Gary Marchionini, *University of North Carolina at Chapel Hill*

Synthesis Lectures on Information Concepts, Retrieval, and Services publishes short books on topics pertaining to information science and applications of technology to information discovery, production, distribution, and management. Potential topics include: data models, indexing theory and algorithms, classification, information architecture, information economics, privacy and identity, scholarly communication, bibliometrics and webometrics, personal information management, human information behavior, digital libraries, archives and preservation, cultural informatics, information retrieval evaluation, data fusion, relevance feedback, recommendation systems, question answering, natural language processing for retrieval, text summarization, multimedia retrieval, multilingual retrieval, and exploratory search.

© Springer Nature Switzerland AG 2022

Reprint of original edition © Morgan & Claypool 2015

All rights reserved. No part of this publication may be reproduced, stored in a retrieval system, or transmitted in any form or by any means—electronic, mechanical, photocopy, recording, or any other except for brief quotations in printed reviews, without the prior permission of the publisher.

On the Efficient Determination of Most Near Neighbors: Horseshoes, Hand Grenades, Web Search, and Other Situations When Close Is Close Enough
Mark S. Manasse

ISBN: 978-3-031-01168-9   paperback
ISBN: 978-3-031-02296-8   ebook

DOI 10.1007/978-3-031-02296-8

A Publication in the Springer series
SYNTHESIS LECTURES ON INFORMATION CONCEPTS, RETRIEVAL, AND SERVICES

Lecture #44
Series Editor: Gary Marchionini, *University of North Carolina at Chapel Hill*
Series ISSN
Synthesis Lectures on Information Concepts, Retrieval, and Services
Print 1947-945X   Electronic 1947-9468

On the Efficient Determination of Most Near Neighbors

Horseshoes, Hand Grenades, Web Search, and
Other Situations When Close Is Close Enough

Second Edition

Mark S. Manasse

*SYNTHESIS LECTURES ON INFORMATION CONCEPTS, RETRIEVAL,
AND SERVICES #44*

ABSTRACT

The time-worn aphorism "close only counts in horseshoes and hand grenades" is clearly inadequate. Close also counts in golf, shuffleboard, archery, darts, curling, and other games of accuracy in which hitting the precise center of the target isn't to be expected every time, or in which we can expect to be driven from the target by skilled opponents.

This book is not devoted to sports discussions, but to efficient algorithms for determining pairs of closely related web pages—and a few other situations in which we have found that inexact matching is good enough — where proximity suffices. We will not, however, attempt to be comprehensive in the investigation of probabilistic algorithms, approximation algorithms, or even techniques for organizing the discovery of nearest neighbors. We are more concerned with finding nearby neighbors; if they are not particularly close by, we are not particularly interested.

In thinking of when approximation is sufficient, remember the oft-told joke about two campers sitting around after dinner. They hear noises coming towards them. One of them reaches for a pair of running shoes, and starts to don them. The second then notes that even with running shoes, they cannot hope to outrun a bear, to which the first notes that most likely the bear will be satiated after catching the slower of them. We seek problems in which we don't need to be faster than the bear, just faster than the others fleeing the bear.

KEYWORDS

nearest neighbor, search algorithms, information retrieval, IR, multi-dimensional

Contents

Forward

Yankee great Yogi Berra said many things that appear to be silly but which time has revealed conceal a greater truth. One phrase attributed to Yogi is this: "when you come to a fork in the road, take it."

For me, I ran into three forks since I first published a book. I arrived at the first and second forks just after I finished final copyediting of the first edition of this book, and sent me off on long paths to determine how best to incorporate the lessons they contained. The third fork was thrust upon me. Thus, the apparent typographic error in the name of this section: these forks spurred my interest in making progress.

The first fork happened when Mikkel Thorup came to visit. He passed along copies of his new paper on twisted tabulation hashing [5]. In the first edition I mentioned his original tabulation hashing work without citation, but found it of little use. The revised version of his paper eliminates (for fixed-length phrase hashing, at least) the value of using Rabin-style CRCs to produce a rolling hash function, which could eliminate the bulk of Section 3.2 as well as some surrounding sections. I will not elaborate on this here, but it is remarkable work and deserves to replace my use of Rabin hashing in efficient implementations.

The second fork was when Ping Li, in response to receiving my book, replied within days with a preprint of the paper he and his students had recently submitted for consideration for a then-impending web conference. In this paper they reexamine the unweighted sampling problem, and use (unbeknownst to them, but well known to Edith Cohen) a partitioning trick used more than 20 years earlier by Flajolet and Martin. As described below, this reduces the running time for unweighted sampling of a document from roughly the product of the length in words of the document and the desired number of produced samples, to just the length of the document. This beautifully simple approach eliminates the need and opportunity for some of the parallel optimizations in the first edition, and led me to wonder if we couldn't find an extension to the weighted variant, which we did, but not without a few detours.

The third fork happened a year ago, when I (and my colleagues) found ourselves in need of new employment, as mentioned in the revised author's biography.

This volume remains largely unchanged at the beginning (correcting a few typos), reflecting a few years ago's state-of-the-art in sampling to approximate Jaccard values. The final chapter provides a slightly more extensive background on tabulation hashing and sample partitioning, followed by an explanation of how we reduce the weighted Jaccard estimation problem to a scaled unweighted problem. We then apply the aforementioned algorithms to produce a slightly biased estimator for weighted similarity.

Foreword to the First Edition

The time-worn aphorism "close only counts in horseshoes and hand grenades," the referent of this book's subtitle, is clearly inadequate. Close also counts in golf, shuffleboard, archery, darts, curling, and other games of accuracy in which hitting the precise center of the target isn't to be expected every time, or in which we can expect to be driven from the target by skilled opponents.

In bicycle stage racing, although the race is won by the fastest to complete all stages, in each stage all finishers in close succession receive the same time for the stage even if the last to finish is a minute behind the first. Consequently, being close is good enough to lose no time in the overall race. The order in which cyclists cross the finishing line counts for points for certain honors and for a stage victory, but it often plays no role in deciding the ultimate honor of winning the full race.

Do these lacunae invalidate our motivating truism, thereby demoting it to possessing merely truthiness? I submit that they do not; rather, we should take them as inspiration to seek other occasions when proximity suffices. For the sports fans among you, thumbing through this volume in hopes of learning techniques for successfully pitching horseshoes, I regret to inform you that the remainder is woefully devoid of any such useful instruction. My knowledge and experience in the delivery of hand grenades is still skimpier. Sports metaphors and discussions of weaponry are almost entirely absent after this point, except for the brief discussion of cross-country running, and ursine ground-speed below.

Those of you hoping for tutorship in finding efficient algorithms for determining pairs of closely related web pages should take heart—this book should be the one for you. Along the way, we will look at a few other situations in which we have found that inexact matching is good enough. We will not, however, attempt to be comprehensive in the investigation of probabilistic algorithms, approximation algorithms, or even techniques for organizing the discovery of nearest neighbors. We are more concerned with finding nearby neighbors; if they are not particularly close by, we are not particularly interested.

In thinking of when approximation is sufficient, remember the oft-told joke about two campers sitting around after dinner. They hear noises coming towards them. One of them reaches for a pair of running shoes, and starts to don them. The other asks if the noise sounded like a bear, and the first affirms that most likely it was a bear. The second then notes that even with running shoes, they cannot hope to outrun a bear, to which the first notes that most likely the bear will be satiated after catching the slower of them. We seek problems in which we don't need to be faster than the bear, just faster than the others fleeing the bear.

Acknowledgments

In this book, when the word "we" occurs, it is neither a regal delusion nor an attempt to include those happy few of you readers in an authorial conspiracy; almost all of the work described herein was originally coauthored with, or inspired by, one or more (listed alphabetically) of the following: Omar Alonso, Nikolaj Bjørner, Andrei Broder, Mike Burrows, Ahmed El-Shimi, Dennis Fetterly, Steve Glassman, Yuri Gurevich, Ran Kalach, Christian König, Ankit Kumar, Jin Li, Ping Li, Frank McSherry, Marc Najork, Greg Nelson, Alex Ntoulas, Adi Oltean, Joe Porkka, Sudipta Sengupta, Vik Singh, Kunal Talwar, Dan Teodosiu, Janet Wiener, and Geoffrey Zweig, not to mention Chuck Thacker, who (as with so many things) helped start it all, and undoubtedly many others who contributed useful ideas in hallway and lunchtime conversations. There are few embedded citations to other works, but I try to credit other authors when describing work first done in papers on which I was not an author.

In addition, this book would be completely unreadable were it not for the skillful and insightful editorial assistance of many of the aforementioned as well as Alex Andoni, Jon Currey, Sergey Ioffe, Malcolm Slaney, and George Varghese. Any remaining lacunae are entirely my fault.

My thanks to everyone mentioned above, to my previous nearby management chain (Mike Schroeder, Roy Levin, and Rick Rashid) for tolerating my spending inordinate amounts of time producing this slim volume, and to my family (especially my wife Janet, and my sons Julian and Declan) and friends for listening to me gripe incessantly about my writing process.

For this second edition, my thanks for conversation and assistance with editing also go to my new colleague, Jeremy Horwitz.

Mark S. Manasse
August 2015

C H A P T E R   1

Introduction

1.1 ON SIMILARITY, RESEMBLANCE, LOOK-ALIKES, AND ENTITY RESOLUTION

For over 2000 years, from Plautus to Shakespeare, from Dumas to Dickens to Twain, from *The Great Dictator* to *Moon over Parador*, from *The Parent Trap* to *Dave*, we have been fascinated and entertained by the humor and drama offered by separated twins, look-alikes, and impersonations. Criminal convictions are often gained through the use of eyewitness testimony, even though DNA evidence has recently freed many people imprisoned due to mistaken identifications by a witness. Resemblance, similarity, and identity should not be conflated.

Medieval philosophers worried about quiddity and haecciety when trying to understand why two identical things were in fact two. Consideration of the statement "Hesperus is Persperus" by Frege made these distinctions somewhat clearer. Kripke showed that this was not necessarily because of any reference to extant objects that were provably the same; we can find meaning in sentences revealing identity, even when the sentence has no referent. For example, "Harry Potter is a student at Hogwarts" seems meaningful, even given our knowledge that neither Harry Potter nor Hogwarts are factual. "The morning star is the evening star" reveals far more than "Venus is Venus," although the referents are the same in both utterances.

Identity can be further confused by design. Remakes, plagiarism, generic drugs, replica watches, and forgeries are a few names for ways in which imitations may attempt to serve in place of an original. *The Front Page* and *His Girl Friday* are clearly distinct films, but both (along with Billy Wilder's remake of *The Front Page* and *Switching Channels*) are screen adaptations of the Hecht and MacArthur play. *The Man Who Knew Too Much* may refer to either of Alfred Hitchcock's thrillers of that name. Rereleases of films with minor modifications lead us to question whether Han shot first in the cantina battle with Greedo in *Star Wars*. Are the later releases no longer the same movie?

When do two recordings of a song differ enough to be considered as not substitutable for one another: when recorded by a different artist, when rereleased from LP to CD, or when converted to a digital format at different bit rates? Serving me a Pepsi when I ask for Coke is plainly fraudulent, but might still slake my thirst. Drug-store brand over-the-counter pharmaceuticals choose names and packaging colors reminiscent of more-heavily advertised brands. Does this masquerade help buyers identify which products are plausible substitutes for others, or does it help to create confusion of identity?

Given two seemingly indistinguishable items, what makes the original more valuable than a copy? A first-edition book more collectible than a reprint? A lithograph worth more than a poster? Perhaps Orson Welles' *F for Fake* asks questions of art forgery best: "Do you think I should confess? To what? Committing masterpieces?"

Returning to purely fictitious matters, I find myself wondering what a Star Trek transporter does to personal identity. Is a reassembled Captain Kirk still captain? By what rights? He shares nothing other than a quantum-level resemblance to the pre-transport captain: no atoms remain, given our limited understanding of how the technology is meant to function. He shares the memories and physical appearance of his prototype, but (as several episodes allow us to conclude) the transporter can assemble more than one such transportee in the same pattern. Which of these should rightly be captain?

President Clinton was clearly sympathetic with some of the difficulties inherent in understanding statements involving the copula: when answering questions about his testimony in a deposition, he stated "that depends on what the meaning of 'is' is."

When is a replica-watch actionable? Is selling a Fauxlex (I use this as an example, because I know of no other fakes with such a euphonious name) timepiece more troubling when it is clearly an homage to the desirability of a Rolex, or when it is sufficiently indistinguishable from an authentic watch as to pass casual inspection for the real piece? What about representing said watch to one's acquaintances as evidence of one's willingness to indulge in minor luxuries, hoping it will pass inspection? What if the watch in question is branded explicitly as "Fauxlex" or "pseudOmega" rather than "Rolex" or "Omega?" Invicta makes many homage-replicas of Rolex watches, proudly displaying their own name and insignia rather than Rolex and their trademark crown. Does the stylistic mimicry make them less artistic? It seems to have freed Invicta to pursue more interesting colors and selections of adornment, safe in knowing that their homage Submariners (Pro Divers) and Daytonas (Speedways) trade at a tenth to a hundredth the price of the actual Rolexes which they resemble.

Fortunately, in this volume, we will concern ourselves with matters of less philosophical import, although occasionally of legal weight. We consider the question of efficiently identifying near-duplicates in large corpora with reasonably high probability, while overlooking few pairs of duplicates and falsely conflating few pairs. Our motivating example comes from the development of Alta Vista, one of the first search engines for the Web. In that application, we sought to eliminate near-duplicate pages from the search web results, to improve the diversity of the list of returned pages. Our studies at the time, and most subsequent investigations, show that roughly a third of all web pages have doppelgangers. Users of a search engine are ill-served when all the results on a page are nearly identical. This issue was first made clear to us when searching for UNIX manual pages; very early in deployment of the Web, nearly every university placed operating system documentation on-line. Adding confusion, the pages had been processed through type-setting software which places the date and organization in the headers and footers on every page, so that the resulting pages, even for descriptions of the same command in the same version of an operating system, are not bit-for-bit identical.

But what makes one web page a near-duplicate of another: textual equivalence, small Hamming distance, the same topic? The inclusion of a single word can dramatically alter the meaning of a document, or not. The replacement of one banner ad by another is unlikely to be relevant to someone searching for words not present in either advertisement.

This book attempts to provide simple means for assessing such matters, and practical algorithms for discovering instances of near-duplication.

In the process, we principally focus on sampling techniques and applications thereof. We will not concern ourselves with exact computations of distance metrics: for meaningful data, there is usually a large divide between things which are close enough and those which are not. For random data in high-dimensional spaces, almost all items which are close enough fall near the boundary. Exact computation can separate these, but is likely to find meaningless differences.

1.2   YOU MUST KNOW AT LEAST THIS MUCH MATH TO READ THIS BOOK

In the section title, I refer to the signs at amusement parks, warning patrons that they must be sufficiently tall that the safety restraint mechanisms are capable of offering protection. In much the same spirit, throughout this work, we depend heavily on probability, and a few ways in which knowledge of probabilistic properties can lead to more efficient algorithms. A smattering of simple knowledge will go a long way; when midway through the book we find ourselves in need of some basic knowledge of group theory, we will introduce the necessary concepts and theorems (mostly without proof). We will focus on algorithms which use probability to select samples from sets, which we can record and compare.

In effect, we hope to gain efficiencies by techniques reminiscent of the old joke in which a new inmate at a prison discovers that the others entertain one another by calling out the numbers pre-assigned to a known collection of jokes. We hope to also save time and effort in generating random outcomes by enumerating all possible outcomes, and then using that enumeration to efficiently select outcomes by number. With luck, unlike in the joke, relating this will not result in your rejection of the message due to incompetent delivery.

There are probabilistic techniques (early examples being those due to Piotr Indyk and Rajeev Motwani; later refined by Moses Charikar and others) providing efficient ways to estimate distances which work using aggregate values, producing only estimates of statistical measures. These techniques generally rely on measures in Euclidean space.

Viewing documents as bags of words, we can interpret them as frequency-weighted vectors in a high-dimensional Euclidean space, with each word contributing a basis vector. We can scale each dimension by the relative importance of each word. A random rotation of this space moves weight fractionally to new dimensions, allowing vectors to be reduced to low dimension by taking the first few dozen coordinates after rotation. This random projection to each dimension can be computed as the inner product of the vector with a randomly chosen unit vector, where each component of the unit vector (following Johnson and Lindenstrauss) can be a scaled selection from a unit Gaussian.

These rotation-based techniques are often referred to by considering the hyperplanes orthogonal to the selected axes. In early expositions on this topic, authors considered extracting individual bits for each axis by computing only on which side of the hyperplane the vector fell. Considering the unit vector in the direction of each rotated axis, this corresponds to deciding whether the inner product of the document vector and a randomly chosen unit vector is positive or negative; this differs from a rotation of all space in that the chosen vectors need not be mutually orthogonal. This makes little difference in practice: random unit vectors in high-dimensional spaces are usually very-nearly orthogonal.

These techniques are efficient, but I prefer sampling approaches because the projections are unyielding: they answer a particular question well, but are difficult to reinterpret to learn answers to other questions. Suppose, for example, that we want to ask what fraction of phrases in a corpus contain the word "the"? With projections, and no further access to the corpus, we cannot answer. With uniform samples, the answer should be roughly the same as the answer in the set of samples.

Some basic concepts from probability theory that we consider next in trying to improve sampling are:

1. cumulative distribution function (CDF) and

2. probability density function (PDF).

1.3   CUMULATIVE DISTRIBUTION AND PROBABILITY DENSITY FUNCTIONS

Suppose we consider a probabilistic event which produces a real-valued outcome. The probability that the outcome is less than all real numbers is zero; the probability that it fails to exceed all real numbers is one. We can represent the cumulative distribution function (CDF) associated with a probability distribution as a mapping from real numbers to the range zero to one, mapping each value v to the least value x such that the total probability of all outcomes less than v is at most x. For the uniform distribution on the unit interval, the CDF is the domain-restricted identity function: the probability that an outcome is at most v is v for v in the unit interval, zero for negative v and one for v larger than one.

If we take two independent trials from two CDFs and consider the maximum of the two values produced, the corresponding CDF is the product of the CDFs, since the outcome falls below v when and only when the outcomes of both trials are less than v. Consequently, the CDF for the maximum of k independent uniform unit samples is v^k, for v in the unit interval; by interpolating, this is true even for arbitrary non-negative real values of k.

Given a CDF, we can select an outcome with matching probability by picking a number x in the unit interval, and finding the least value v for which the CDF equals or exceeds x. Since the

CDF is monotone increasing, this inverse function exists, and is continuous except where some particular outcome has a positive probability (and thus infinite density) of selection. In some cases we may be able to find the inverse function analytically (for the maximum of k uniform choices, the inverse function is $\sqrt[k]{x}$). For other CDFs, we may need to use binary search, or some other approximation technique to find the inverse.

In some cases, we present techniques that relate two CDFs, and avoid some inversions by noting that, even using a crude approximation, the outcome is guaranteed to be dominated by some previously evaluated outcome.

In cases where the CDF is very smooth, we can also look at the probability density function (PDF) associated with the CDF, which is the derivative of the CDF. For the uniform distribution, the PDF is constantly one in the unit interval, and zero outside. No precise analog exists in the discrete case, where all the probability mass is concentrated on the finite set of available outcomes; in this case, the more naïve notion of each outcome having a fixed probability of occurrence will be employed.

We will sometimes use the complementary CDF (CCDF) in place of the CDF; this is just one minus the CDF, and thus also ranges between zero and one, but represents the probability of a random value being larger than a specified value. CCDFs are monotone decreasing and invertible.

CHAPTER 2

Comparing Web Pages for Similarity: An Overview

When comparing pages in a corpus, there are some things one has to consider (which we do in the following sections).

1. What are the features of a web page which are to be compared?

2. Can we use numbers instead of strings to represent features?

3. What comparison or metric should we use to measure proximity of features?

4. Given that corpora typically contain billions of pages and petabytes of content, what should we do to reduce the features of a corpus to a manageable size?

5. Having chosen features, a metric, and a (probably lossy) compression scheme, how do we find most of the pairs of web pages which neighbor one another?

The next few sections provide brief introductions to each of these. We return to them all in much greater depth in the sections that follow.

2.1 CHOOSING THE FEATURES OF A WEB PAGE TO COMPARE

There are many things we can use in text files to define *features* (and many other ways to define features in non-text files; some recent papers have shown great success using geometric relationships between landmark points in images to locate similar images; several of these papers have used similarity-estimation techniques rather like the ones we explain).

In comparing general HTML documents, we have had success using very simple features: strip away all non-text markup from a document (such as font changes and other HTML tags), fold case (in language encodings that support upper and lower case), make characters as canonical as possible (normalizing Unicode to a particular representation, for example), and turn all word delimiters (white-space, punctuation, and the like) into a fixed single delimiter. Then consider all sequences (*phrases*) of five (for some value of "five") consecutive words, including (so that the words of a document are in one-to-one correspondence to the phrases) five-word sequences where a few of the words occur at the end of the document, and the remainder at the beginning. If that last part seems inelegant to you, skip it; we introduce it primarily so that we can use a single value to indicate both the length of a document in words and the number of features it contains, but we will not often need to refer to both at the same time.

If you feel so inclined, you might choose to remember enough of the HTML markup to take note of important boundary markers (headings, paragraphs, titles, divisions, and the like), and use this as clues that certain parts of the page are more important than other parts; this may come in handy when we consider weighted similarity later; we may also want to see if any of our features are repeated within a document or are shared by other documents, so that we can pick a weight proportional to the replication count, or, as is more common in TF-IDF weighting, the logarithm of the frequency of occurrence. The acronym *TF-IDF* expands to *term-frequency (multiplied by) inverse document frequency*, which is to say that you take the number of occurrences in your document divided by the number of occurrences of the feature in your entire corpus (or some approximation thereto, possibly derived by sampling).

Other authors have considered other kinds of features. Most approaches using Euclidean distance consider just the unigrams, that is, the individual words as features, viewing a document as a vector where the axes are all the words in your dictionary, and the length in each dimension is the weight assigned to the corresponding word.

Some authors, when considering news articles, have observed that headlines of news stories are quite terse, usually omitting stop words such as definite articles. Moreover, breaking news stories quite often are recast by wire services several times per day, as more details and expert comments become available. As a consequence, de-duplication of news stories is challenging (due to the repeated emendation of the story), and useful to the reader (in order to read only the fresh content on some newsworthy topic). Studies (the Theobald el al. *SpotSigs* paper, for example) have found better results looking at only those phrases containing or even beginning with stop words, since the emendations often preserve most of the content of the story, while changing the headlines, captions, and the lead; additionally, the headlines are often replaced by newspapers with ones that better fit the available space, the editor's sense of humor, and their local readers, even while preserving the content of a wire story. Identifying the evolving versions of a story can allow an automated clipping service to recognize the equivalence of a story appearing on the wire, and in both a national and a local newspaper.

Having chosen the raw features, we may then apply a further mapping, to convert the features into numbers of a fixed size, so that our world is more uniform in size. In many of our experiments, we have chosen to use Rabin hashing (a form of cyclic redundancy code) to convert features into 64-bit (or longer) integers. Rabin fingerprints have a few virtues we consider later, among which are a provable probability of collisions, and an algebraic structure that simplifies the computation of a sliding window of hash values.

Several authors have investigated some interesting techniques for image comparison, but these are beyond the author's personal knowledge and ability to describe, other than in vague generalities. The basic idea is to locate points in the image which bear some interesting geometric relationship to one another. This relationship should be unchanged under transformations viewed as inessential, such as scaling, minor rotation, cropping that preserves the points of interest, color saturation, and other transforms expected in the re-use of the image. From these relationships, we label them with a mostly invariant mapping, and use similarity techniques on the resulting streams, as elsewhere.

2.2   TURNING FEATURES INTO INTEGERS (RABIN HASHING)

No matter how we choose to slice up a document to produce features, it is often convenient for the features to be represented by fixed-length integers instead of as strings, to facilitate manipulation. To help with this, we often replace the features by a simple hash of the constituents of the features. We often use Rabin's variant on cyclic redundancy codes for this, because of a few special properties.

1. Rabin fingerprints have good anti-collision properties; in particular, when using a k-bit Rabin fingerprint, strings which differ by at most k consecutive bits will have different fingerprints.

2. Rabin fingerprints cope well with simple systematic variation: all extensions by appending up to 2^k zero bits to a string produce differing fingerprints.

3. Rabin fingerprints can be concatenated; knowing the length of a string A, and the fingerprints of strings A and B, we can compute the fingerprint of string AB, the concatenation of the strings.

4. Rabin fingerprints adapt well to sliding windows: removing the initial bytes from a string, and appending a few more bytes can be done efficiently.

Mathematically, a Rabin fingerprint is obtained by treating a string as a polynomial with Boolean coefficients. We then prepend a leading 1 to the polynomial (so that different lengths of runs of zeros are distinguishable; in some applications discovering long strings of zeros is useful, and we can skip this step), and append k trailing zeros, so that numerically-consecutive strings have well-separated fingerprints. We then find the residue modulo a preselected primitive polynomial.

As an example of Rabin fingerprints, the polynomial $p = x^8 + x^4 + x^3 + x^2 + 1$ is primitive of degree 8 in $GF(2)[x]$. The character A in ASCII has the value $65_{10} = 41_{16}$, so the polynomial corresponding to "A" (including prepending a leading one, and appending 8 trailing zeros to match the degree of p) is $x^{16} + x^{14} + x^8$. Modulo p, $x^{16} + x^{14} + x^8 \equiv x^{14} + x^{12} + x^{11} + x^{10} \equiv x^{12} + x^{11} + x^9 + x^8 + x^6 \equiv x^{11} + x^9 + x^7 + x^4 \equiv x^9 + x^6 + x^5 + x^4 + x^3 \equiv x^6 + x$. Thus, 42_{16} is the hash value.

Primitivity implies irreducibility, which gives us some collision-resistance; a polynomial p is *primitive* when the remainders after dividing by p of the multiplicative powers of the polynomial

x generate the multiplicative group of the Galois field, which ensures that we can append $2^k - 1$ zeros before we generate a collision. We'll return to this, with some sample code, later on; before we do, we want to note that Rabin fingerprints are useful, and mathematically quite simple. Correspondingly, we feel obligated to provide a few general warnings about things one should not do with them.

1. Do not compute the fingerprint of a fingerprint using the same polynomials; the differences are intrinsically related to the given polynomial, so collisions are far more common than one might like.

2. Expect that the fingerprints of algebraically related strings will also be related algebraically. The fingerprinting process is linear: addition of Boolean polynomials is just bit-wise inequality, and if A, B, C, D are strings where $A + B = C + D$, then $f(A) + f(B) = f(C) + f(D)$, where f is the fingerprinting function. All too often (if, for example, the strings are URLs from a pair of mirror websites) the strings will differ systematically—the hostnames of URLs from the same site will match and cancel, and the paths will agree except for the specific file name.

3. Fingerprinting is not cryptographic: on random or sequential data one should expect collisions to be rare, but it is easy to construct strings which will collide, given knowledge of the polynomial, or access to a small number of selected input and output pairs.

2.3 HOW SHOULD WE MEASURE THE PROXIMITY OF FEATURES?

Having chosen a feature abstraction technique, we next decide how close two bundles of features are. Generally, one chooses to view the set of features of a document as unordered, with any sequencing having been performed at feature generation. Viewing the collection of features as a set (or multi-set, if there are repeated features), the usual choices are to view *proximity* using either an ℓ_1 (Manhattan distance) or ℓ_2 (Euclidean distance) norm, or to look at cosine similarity (which imposes scale-invariance on Euclidean distances), or the Jaccard coefficient (which brings some scale-invariance to Manhattan distance).

To remind the reader of a few basic terms, Manhattan distance between two points is the sum of the absolute values of the coordinate-wise difference, while Euclidean distance is the square root of the sum of the squares of the coordinate-wise differences. For 0-1 vectors, the Manhattan distance is also the Hamming distance of the corresponding strings of bits. Levenshtein distance is a related concept for strings, which allows insertion and deletion as well as replacement, and is usually applied to strings of characters rather than bits. As with many things peripherally related to this text, we advise the interested reader to consult *Wikipedia*.

More precisely, the ℓ_1 norm for distance between two vectors u, v is the sum of the absolute values of the term-wise difference:

$$\ell_1(u, v) = \|u - v\|_1 = \sum_i |u_i - v_i| .$$

The Euclidean ℓ_2 distance is the standard Pythagorean formula-derived

$$\ell_2(u, v) = \|u - v\|_2 = \sqrt{\sum_i (u_i - v_i)^2} .$$

More general norms will not be considered in this volume.

Comparing vectors, we may choose to consider only the directions in which the vectors point. In doing so, we can compute a number between -1 and 1, ranging from completely opposite in direction to in complete agreement, with zero representing orthogonality. One way to do this is to look at the cosine of the angle separating the two vectors, which is easily computed—if we recall our trigonometry lessons, the inner product of two vectors is equal to the cosine of the angle between the two vectors multiplied by the Euclidean length of each vector: $u \cdot v = \|u\|_2 \|v\|_2 \cos \angle uv$. For unit-length vectors, the inner product directly yields the cosine of the angle between the vectors. We often consider *similarity* instead of distance, where similarity is one minus distance (for scaled-measures of distance).

The Jaccard coefficient or similarity of two sets of features is only slightly more complicated, and is often better-suited for comparing large vectors in an ℓ_1-like style: for sets (or, equivalently, vectors with values of 0 and 1) we consider the amount of agreement divided by the total number of features in the union of the two sets:

$$J(u, v) = \frac{|u \cap v|}{|u \cup v|} .$$

For 0-1 valued vectors, $\min(u, v)$ equals 1 when both values are 1, that is, where the corresponding sets intersect, while $\max(u, v)$ equals 1 when either value is 1, thus in exactly the union. Both are zero elsewhere, so we can write

$$J(u, v) = \frac{\sum_i \min(u_i, v_i)}{\sum_i \max(u_i, v_i)} = \frac{\|\min(u, v)\|_1}{\|\max(u, v)\|_1} .$$

This formulation can be applied to arbitrary non-negative vectors, giving us a weighted Jaccard coefficient where the weights are arbitrary non-negative values. We can relate the Jaccard coefficient to the ℓ_1-norm following Sergey Ioffe in observing that, for non-negative values of a and b,

$$\min(a, b) = \frac{a + b - |a - b|}{2}$$

while

$$\max(a, b) = \frac{a + b + |a - b|}{2} .$$

As a consequence,

$$J(u,v) = \frac{\|\min(u,v)\|_1}{\|\max(u,v)\|_1} = \frac{\frac{\|u\|_1 + \|v\|_1 - \|u-v\|_1}{2}}{\frac{\|u\|_1 + \|v\|_1 + \|u-v\|_1}{2}} = \frac{\|u\|_1 + \|v\|_1 - \|u-v\|_1}{\|u\|_1 + \|v\|_1 + \|u-v\|_1}.$$

Given $\|u\|_1$, $\|v\|_1$, and $J(u,v)$, we can solve for $\|u-v\|_1$ as

$$\|u-v\|_1 = \frac{1 - J(u,v)}{1 + J(u,v)} (\|u\|_1 + \|v\|_1).$$

In this way, we can store only the one-norms of a collection, together with a good way to estimate Jaccard similarities and Manhattan distances, as first noted by Shmoys, Tardos, and Aardal. Consequently, we address only the problem of estimating Jaccard coefficients hereinafter.

2.4   FEATURE REDUCTION

Given that corpora typically contain billions of pages and petabytes of content, what can we do to reduce the set of features of a corpus to a manageable size? In this section we address this question by considering consistent sampling techniques, and show that they can provide accurate estimations the degree of similarity.

For comparisons using the Jaccard coefficient, we can hope to find good ways to estimate the Jaccard coefficient through sampling. In what we consider later in this book, we find that we can get good estimates by choosing samples a and b from sets A and B so that $P(a = b) = J(A,B)$; by picking multiple independent samples, the fraction of samples which match is a good estimator for the Jaccard similarity. Such a collection of samples is often referred to as a *sketch*.

As we examine later, selecting samples that estimate Jaccard for unweighted sets is only a little tricky (and the techniques for doing so have improved greatly over the years); selecting samples that estimate weighted Jaccard is a bit harder, although recent advances have made it quite feasible.

We may find (as Li and König first suggested) that retaining even a few hundred samples is burdensome; beginning in the Teodosiu et al. Remote Differential Compression work (described far below), and continuing until quite recently, we have found that choosing weakened approximations to samples can be quite effective. If, for example, our features consist of fragments of text of length averaging 100 bytes, storing 100 samples would occupy 10 kilobytes of memory. If, instead, we choose 200 samples, but retain only a single bit from each one (after applying suitable rerandomization), we expect that purely due to dumb luck, 100 of our 200 bits will match even given completely unrelated text, while the other 100 will reflect the underlying similarity. Of course, we cannot know which 100 bits will match by dumb luck (and that may be an overestimate: if the true similarity of two files is quite high, many of the bits will match for a very good reason, having nothing to do with the sample reduction).

In general, if two files have Jaccard coefficient J and we compute samples a_i, b_i from each file and then map each sample to k bits using a random mapping f_i (different mappings for different i, so as to not repeat accidental collisions), we expect that $Q \triangleq P(a_i = b_i) = J + \frac{1-J}{2^k} = \frac{1}{2^k} + (1 - \frac{1}{2^k})J$; the second term in the first sum is the probability of agreement due to luck alone. Solving for J, we find $J = \frac{Q - \frac{1}{2^k}}{1 - \frac{1}{2^k}} = \frac{2^k Q - 1}{2^k - 1}$; this is not quite as simple as computing J from high-precision samples, but considerably more storage-efficient for small values of k, needing only $n \triangleq ik$ bits to record a sketch, instead of $64i$, assuming we can accurately represent a sample in 64 bits; we will probably want to increase i slightly to deal with the loss of precision for small k (for example, we should roughly double the number of samples when $k = 1$).

One drawback is that the stored samples are no longer actual samples; they are now intelligible to the untrained observer only as good reasons why the two files might be considered to be similar. With luck, the space savings of a factor of roughly 30 for comparable levels of accuracy justifies the loss of simplicity.

In cases where only high-degree similarity is of interest, the next section describes an alternative compression scheme, for recording and comparing samples in bulk.

2.5   PUTTING IT TOGETHER WITH SUPERSHINGLING

Having chosen features, a metric, and a lossy compression scheme, how do we locate most of the pairs of web pages which neighbor one another?

In most situations, one cares only to find neighbors that are close: for instance, in looking at neighborhood patterns of common illnesses, we are more likely to be concerned when the neighbors are next door than we are when they are five miles away. Knowing which web page is most similar to a given page might satisfy some basic curiosity, but it is of less immediate interest than knowing that two of the pages which are to be returned as query results are nearly identical.

Given a list of samples (or suitably truncated samples), the remaining problem is to find those pairs of sets which closely resemble one another. After some empirical study, we found that users are usually happy to accept that pages with a Jaccard similarity of at least 0.95 are near-duplicates when using modest-length phrases as features. These users are generally willing to concede that pages with a Jaccard similarity below 0.75 are distinguishable. Accordingly, we looked for efficient techniques which would almost always discover pages with high similarity, and usually ignore those with low similarity.

In working with Alta Vista, we settled on collecting 84 samples from each page. We grouped these samples into 6 sets of 14 samples, and then applied a hash function to each set. This resulted in each web page engendering six values. Consider two documents with a true Jaccard similarity of 0.95 or larger. The probability that 14 samples in a row all match is then $0.95^{14} \approx 0.5$ (this rough numerical coincidence was largely why we chose numbers like 6, 14, and 84). At similarity 0.95, at least 2 of the 6 values should agree at least 87% of the time; were the true Jaccard similarity less than 0.75 then the likelihood of 2 or more matches would be smaller than $1\frac{1}{2}\%$. These compressed values, for largely historical reasons, are often referred to as *supershingles* (because the overlapping sequences of words constituting features reminded us of shingles forming a roof, and supershingles are much more expressive than individual shingles).

Various other combinations also work. When using the bit reductions described in the previous section, we can look for strings at small Hamming distance to one another. One moderately efficient technique here is to break the string into small segments, of length perhaps ten, index the segments that occur, and those at Hamming distance one from each segment. This would expand the storage requirements for an index by a factor of 11, but make lookups fast; if space is more costly than computation time, we could do the reverse, and look up all 11 strings with at most one bit differing from the segment presented.

If we have strings of length 200, this would produce 20 segments. At similarity 0.5, we expect $\frac{3}{4}$ of the bits in each segment to match, so at least 9 of 10 bits should match over $\frac{1}{5}$ of the time. With 20 segments to check, we expect to find roughly 4 matching (or near-matching) segments.

CHAPTER 3

A Personal History of Web Search

In 1995, just prior to public release, we discovered a problem with the Alta Vista search engine: most of the time searching worked just fine, but sometimes the results were highly repetitive. We knew that the search engine would not always present the best answer first, so Alta Vista would offer ten different URLs as potential answers to each query. Usually, these answers were varied and diverse, so that a query for "jaguar" might produce suggestions ranging from animals to cars to computer operating systems. We considered this good: given an ambiguous query, it seemed better to offer the user diversity: a few choices that spanned the gamut of possible meanings. Sometimes, however, Alta Vista presented ten answers almost all the same. This happened surprisingly often on the queries issued by the designers of Alta Vista, since a significant fraction of those queries were to locate manual pages for UNIX commands. Early in the history of the Web, programmers had constructed automated tools for converting UNIX manual pages into web pages; the UNIX formatting tool placed the institution name and the current date in the footer and header of the pages so constructed, and these had been preserved in the conversion to HTML. Sadly, this meant that every manual page was represented by multiple copies in the corpus, any one of which would have satisfied the user's information need; the second copy, sad to say, afforded the user little additional value beyond the first, other than accessibility.

Alta Vista had seen a related problem before: many web sites are mirrored for performance, or available via multiple URLs to simplify the organization of websites. In these cases, the copies are usually exact duplicates: the returned pages are byte-for-byte equivalent. Computer scientists have long had techniques that can handle duplication: fingerprints or checksums can provide probabilistic tests that make it impossible for duplicate values to be returned, while making it highly improbable that unique content gets erroneously marked as a duplicate. What was needed was a hashing technique that could efficiently flag approximate- or near-duplicates so that we could increase diversity by eliminating near-duplicate results.

What we came up with was an instance of what became known (thanks to Piotr Indyk and Rajeev Motwani) as *locality-sensitive hashing*: a hash function whose result usually stays largely unchanged when the input is largely unchanged. The particular technique we found became known as *min-hashing*. We looked at a variety of distance measures, and chose to estimate the *Jaccard coefficient* of pairs of documents.

Making sense of this requires a little more background. Web pages are formatted using HTML, a markup language which allows text to have sizes and font styles, and to include paragraph breaks, headers, and titles. While someone learning HTML might be interested in finding examples of ways to use the text-formatting features of HTML, Alta Vista decided that, for purposes of duplicate detection, it sufficed to consider only the visible text. Thus, the first step in duplicate elimination is *normalization*: in our case, the reduction of the HTML input to its static visual content, ignoring many additional features such as font, capitalization, punctuation, embedded images, and other things that leave the basic text intact. Alta Vista further chose to break the running text into punctuation or white-space delimited words. The choice of normalization is critical; recent papers (such as Theobald et al.) have considered normalization that captures only punctuation or extremely popular words, and found these useful in some application domains.

The next step is *feature selection*: combining normalized values into small groups which are, one hopes, more specific to particular input values. For Alta Vista, we chose to assemble short phrases of consecutive words, including overlap. This meant that, given the original text `Now is the time for all good men`, the three-word phrase set after normalization might be {`now is the`, `is the time`, `the time for`, `time for all`, `for all good`, `all good men`}. Again, the choice of three consecutive words rather than five is for illustration only. Alta Vista went a little further: to make the number of phrases match the number of words, we imagined that the words at the end were followed by the words at the beginning; in our example, we would also have had the phrases `good men now` and `men now is`, which meant that the title words which begin web pages appear in just as many phrases as other words. An alternative choice would have been to allow shortened phrases at the beginning and end of documents. We ran some experiments, and decided that looped documents were slightly better, and that this primarily mattered in very short documents, where a large fraction of the phrases are looped.

Treating the feature set as a set rather than as a bag was a decision we made largely for expedience: most documents other than children's books don't have many repeated phrases of five or more words. This choice does reduce our ability to distinguish individual pages of many Dr. Seuss books from the whole, but our initial target set of users for Alta Vista could most likely identify the source of phrases such as "I do not like green eggs and ham" without our assistance. We will allow for comparing multiplicity later; at the time, our best idea was to tag phrases with an instance number, making each instance unique, but we will see how to do better.

Next, we choose a *distance* function d: a measurement for assessing how close two feature sets are. For the kinds of approximation techniques we considered, we wanted this measure to have many (but not necessarily all) of the properties of a *metric*: for all feature sets A and B,

1. $d(A, B) = d(B, A)$ and

2. $d(A, A) = 0$.

We also chose one property not typical of metrics, listed below, while ignoring a standard property of metrics, namely the triangle inequality.

3. $0 \le d(A, B) \le 1$.

This last property makes distances and probabilities interchangeable.

Given these, an *unbiased estimator* for a distance function d is a family of mappings which, given a set A, produce a sample value $s(A)$ for A in a space with a sample distance function f such that

$$d(A, B) = E(f(s(A), s(B))) .$$

That is, the expected distance between $s(A)$ and $s(B)$, averaged over all members of the family, should equal the actual distance. Since the value $s(A)$ depends only on A and the choice of mapping, rather than computing the average, we can fix a random subset of the family, and produce all of the values $a(A)$ for all features f in the subset. Recall that we call such a sequence of values a sketch, and prove that under certain kinds of distance functions, and certain families of mappings, that these sketches give rise to an unbiased estimator.

For Alta Vista, for d we chose the Jaccard distance (defined above) as our distance function. Recall that the Jaccard distance between two sets equals the ratio of the cardinality of the elements unique to either of the two sets and the cardinality of the union of the two sets; it may be easier to think about the Jaccard coefficient instead, which is the cardinality of the intersection divided by the cardinality of the union.

Again, as equations, the Jaccard coefficient for sets A and B is

$$J(A, B) = \frac{\|A \cap B\|}{\|A \cup B\|}$$

and the Jaccard distance is

$$J_\delta(A, B) = 1 - \frac{\|A \cap B\|}{\|A \cup B\|} = \frac{\|A \cup B\| - \|A \cap B\|}{\|A \cup B\|} = \frac{\|A \Delta B\|}{\|A \cup B\|} ,$$

where Δ is the symmetric difference function for sets.

To estimate the Jaccard coefficient, choose a random element *uniformly* (that is, with equal probability for all) from A as $v(A)$ and set the sample distance function f to be a functional representation of *Kronecker's delta*:

$$f(x, y) = \begin{cases} 1 & \text{if } x = y \\ 0, & \text{otherwise} . \end{cases}$$

Suppose further that the selection function $s(A)$ has a simple consistency policy: if $s(A \cup B) \in A$, then $s(A) = s(A \cup B)$; in other words, the sampled value doesn't change when restricting to a subset unless it must. In that case, averaging over all consistent uniform selection functions, the probability of picking the same samples is the Jaccard coefficient.

Proof. Even though $s(A)$ and $s(B)$ are computed independently, imagine that we had $A \cup B$ available to us. $s(A \cup B)$ is a uniformly random element of the union. It must be an element of A, B, or both. At least one of $s(A)$ and $s(B)$ equals $s(A \cup B)$, by consistency; when (and only when) $s(A \cup B)$ is in both A and B can we have $s(A) = s(B)$. The probability of a uniformly selected random element of the union falling into the intersection is exactly the Jaccard coefficient.

Note that we can compute the Jaccard distance by taking one minus the Jaccard coefficient; to fit into the formalism, replace the Kronecker delta with its opposite, that is, estimate the probability that the samples differ.

Our remaining problem here is to pick an element uniformly for A consistent with a uniform choice from $A \cup B$, without knowledge of B. This is where *min-hashing* comes in.

Pick a *valuation* mapping, μ, mapping elements of our sets in a one-to-one way to some well-ordered set, that is, an ordered set in which every subset contains a least element. Mapping to ordinals would work; mapping to any finite ordered set will also work when our universe is finite (which it is likely to be, in practice, since infinite universes are computationally intractable). Suppose that this coefficient mapping μ is chosen randomly from all functions with the same domain and range. Having fixed on μ, we can select $v_\mu(A)$ to be that element x from A for which $\mu(x)$ is smallest. Since the range of μ is well ordered, there is a smallest value. Since μ is one-to-one, there can be only one x which results in that value. This is often written using *argmin*: for one-to-one functions and well-ordered ranges (or finite inputs) to guarantee that this is well defined, $\operatorname{argmin}_{x \in A}(\mu(x))$, is the unique element producing the minimal valuation. The result of argmin is also referrred to as the *pre-image* of the selected value.

Averaged over all such valuation functions, $s(A)$ is a uniformly random selection from A. This construction gives us consistency as well: the element of $A \cup B$ with smallest image after applying a pseudo-random mapping, if it is an element of A, still has the smallest image when considering only elements of A. Thus, selecting a sample by taking the argmin (remember, the argument to the chosen mapping function which results in the minimal output) of a randomly chosen one-to-one mapping to a well-ordered set produces samples which match with probability precisely equal to the Jaccard similarity of the original sets.

This is, of course, only on average; for a specific choice of mapping and a given pair of sets, the samples either match or not. To get a better estimation of the similarity, we can repeat this experiment by picking more mappings, or we can try to find a good way to choose more samples using a single mapping.

Choosing more mappings has some nice properties: if the mappings are chosen independently, this results in sampling with replacement: an element can be chosen multiple times by different valuation mappings. If the Jaccard similarity of two sets is p, then the probability of matching k consecutive samples drawn independently with replacement is simply p^k.

There are several ways to choose multiple samples using the same function, with differing utility. We can consider not just the element with smallest image, but, say, the 100 elements with the 100 smallest images, for sets containing at least 100 elements, or the complete set, for smaller sets (by choosing the elements with the 100 smallest images, we are sampling without replacement). We can choose some property of the values, and take all inputs for which the image has that property; for example, if the images are positive integers, we might choose all those evenly divisible by some power of two. Both of these still lead to a consistent set of samples: after reducing the input set, all elements which remain in the set which were chosen for the full set will continue to be chosen. With reasonable mapping functions and properties, all elements are still equally likely to be in the sample set. An example of an unreasonable map and property combination would be a hash function uniformly producing only odd values, and a selection function choosing samples with mapped value divisible by 32; this combination patently would not work.

When taking multiple selections, we have to revise our technique for computing how these samples approximate Jaccard similarity. Given a consistent and uniform set-valued sampling function s, and two sets A and B, the Jaccard similarity

$$J(A, B) = \frac{\|A \cap B\|}{\|A \cup B\|} = E\left(\frac{\|A \cap B \cap C\|}{\|C\|}\right)$$

when computing expectation over uniformly selected non-empty random subsets C of $A \cup B$. But $s(A \cup B)$ is a uniformly random subset of $A \cup B$, and, by consistency, $s(A) \cap s(A \cup B) = A \cap s(A \cup B)$, and $s(A \cup B) = s(s(A) \cup s(B))$. Therefore,

$$\frac{\|A \cap B \cap s(A \cup B)\|}{\|s(A \cup B)\|} = \frac{\|s(A) \cap s(B) \cap s(A \cup B)\|}{\|s(A \cup B)\|} = \frac{\|s(A) \cap s(B) \cap s(s(A) \cup s(B))\|}{\|s(s(A) \cup s(B))\|} .$$

Now, $s(A \cup B)$ is a uniform random subset of $A \cup B$, when averaged over all s. We can thus fix a random selection function s, and compute $s(A)$ for all sets A. We still need to be able to compute $s(s(A) \cup s(B))$ given only $s(A)$ and $s(B)$, but for many selection functions this is relatively easy. Having precomputed these samples, we can, without bias, estimate $J(A, B)$ as:

$$J(A, B) \approx \frac{\|s(A) \cap s(B) \cap s(s(A) \cup s(B))\|}{\|s(s(A) \cup s(B))\|}$$

without knowledge of A, B or the universe of all sets (but with knowledge of the samples $s(A)$ and $s(B)$).

At Alta Vista, we used only fixed-sized sampling (that is, multiple sampling functions where $\|s(A)\| = 1$ for all A), after discovering that the alternatives make the computation of supershingles (see below) difficult, although some progress has been made recently in this area.

For proportional-sized sampling, using, say, linear congruence (where we ask that the random value be divisible by one hundred, say), $s(s(A) \cup s(B)) = s(A) \cup s(B)$, which reduces the computation to:

$$J(A, B) \approx \frac{\|s(A) \cap s(B)\|}{\|s(A) \cup s(B)\|} .$$

For smallest-k, where we select the pre-images of the k smallest values, a bit more work is required. We have to exclude those elements that had no chance of being selected in the union, despite being chosen in one or both sets individually. For example, some element may have the fifth smallest image in each of two sets, but fail to have small enough image to finish better than ninth in the union. This cannot happen when we choose only the smallest image element; the very smallest in a union of sets is the very smallest in at least one component of the union. In the k-smallest setting, we are forced to keep the full complexity for computing minima, restricting computations to only those elements which are relatively small in the union of the relatively small.

3.1   COMPLEXITY ISSUES AND IMPLEMENTATION

In the smallest-k setting, things are about as computationally efficient as they can be, subject to picking good sampling functions. You may want to keep the sampled elements in sorted order, to simplify the union and intersection operators as merges, or you may prefer to use hash-based intersections, depending on your expectations about the size of the sets and the value of similarity. Several authors have considered the effects of using reduced families of functions from which to select your sampling function; the term *min-wise independence* should help you find papers on this. We refer the interested reader to a search engine in this case, because we will assume true randomness throughout this volume.

While single-selection using multiple functions may appear to be less efficient (because multiple valuation functions have to computed for each feature), it has benefits that may outweigh those deficiencies. First, when looking for *near neighbors*, we want to restrict our attention to those neighbors with a Jaccard similarity, or *Jaccard index* exceeding some threshold. If, for instance, that threshold is 0.95, consider that $0.95^{14} = 0.48767497911552985900087890625 \approx 0.5$. Thus, if we take 14 samples using 14 selection functions from 2 sets with Jaccard index 0.95, the probability of them all agreeing is roughly $\frac{1}{2}$. Empirical testing by Alta Vista confirmed, for certain choices of feature generation, and for most documents, that a threshold of 0.95 was often a reasonable match to human judgments as to whether 2 pages were near-duplicates of one another.

By computing a hash function of a set of 14 pre-images, we can compute what is historically known as a *supershingle*, and we can retain only a small set of these supershingles for each document. In Alta Vista, we chose to do this, and to compute only 6 supershingles for each document. We would expect roughly 3 of these 6 to match for documents with Jaccard index of 0.95; to increase recall with little reduction in precision, we asked for at least 2 of the 6 to match in order to consider documents as good candidates to be deemed near-duplicates. We reduced the computational work still more by noting that there are only 15 ways to choose a pair from 6 supershingles. For that reason, we then computed 15 hash tables, one for each pair, containing the corresponding paired supershingle values. Any collision in any of the tables would suggest, barring accidental hash collisions, that the corresponding documents had two matching supershingles. We chose hash functions which, given the size of the Alta Vista corpus at the time, led us to believe that the number of accidental collisions would be greatly outnumbered by the number of near-duplicates. These computational and storage efficiencies allow us to build systems that have scaled well as corpora have grown from tens of millions of documents to tens of billions.

Simple application of the binomial theorem allows us to compute the probability of having at least two supershingle matches as a function of the true Jaccard index, as displayed in Figure 3.1. In Figure 3.2, we see the same graph, but with the y-axis displayed using a logarithmic scale, making it easier to appreciate that the probability of declaring that two documents with a Jaccard similarity of 0.7 are near-duplicates is just under one in a thousand.

Empirically, we found that most pairs of documents are almost entirely dissimilar (Jaccard < 0.1), and that the misidentification rate is often low enough even without a verification pass, an observation which seems to still be largely valid. When applied to corpus simplification, a simple connected-component clustering sufficed, particularly as the similarity threshold was large. It should be noted that this will lead to some misclassification; Jaccard neighbors are neighbors in a scaled l_1 ball in high-dimensional space, where, in the standard phrase-based feature model, each distinct phrase is a dimension. In such a ball, almost all the volume is very near the boundary, so we expect (and find) that any clustering on random data is extremely sensitive to changes in the choice of selection functions. Random points in a high-dimensional sphere are mostly found near the border of the sphere. But actual web pages are not random, so this works out in practice.

When using proportional or min-k sampling, clustering near neighbors is more complicated than using supershingles. We cannot expect significant runs of identical selections except at very high levels of similarity. In proportional sampling, variations in document length limit any statistical technique's effectiveness by greatly reducing the expected Jaccard index. Pruning techniques are of some help here, if we use a second grouping technique to fix alignment issues between sets of samples. If, for instance, we choose a hash function of our samples with a 10% probability of returning a value of zero, and partition ordered sets of samples at such places, we would expect roughly 100 samples to divide into 10 groups of roughly 10 samples each, so that at Jaccard index 0.95, there should be a fair chance that at least one such group would match exactly.

Sampling in this way is far more parsimonious in using randomness: we choose a single selection function, evaluate it on all of our features, and choose the smallest, or all the ones which are sufficiently lucky. The choice of that selection function derandomizes the process, and reduces selection to a single function evaluation per feature. If we are considering all pairs of documents, the computation of Jaccard similarity with min-k samples is straightforward (although there is a small adjustment described above) that must be made to reduce both sample sets to the elements contained in the min-k of the union of the documents. Our inability to use supershingling and escape from comparing all pairs in this setting pushes our quest for efficiency in a different direction, however.

3.2 IMPLEMENTING DUPLICATE SUPPRESSION

Turning away from the theory of well orderings, we note that, in the world of practical computations, we can safely ignore infinite inputs (as search engines extend their reach ever farther into the expanding Web, we should not ignore the possibility of arbitrary large, but finite, input). Instead, we can find simple functions mapping without repetition into total orderings, secure in the

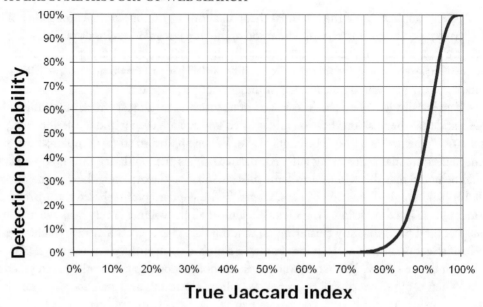

Figure 3.1: Jaccard index vs. probability of two matching supershingles, linear scale.

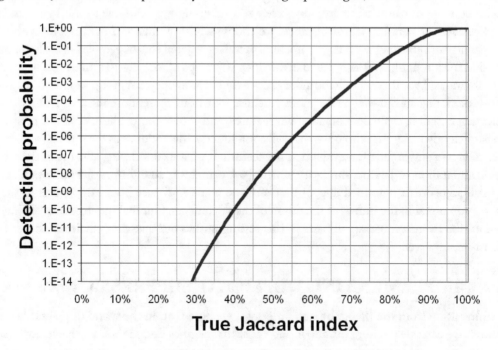

Figure 3.2: Jaccard index vs. probability of two matching supershingles, logarithmic scale.

knowledge that in any finite ordered collection, there will be a unique smallest—finite orderings *must* be well-ordered.

The most naïve sampling loop for multiple-function min-hashing (all the code samples that follow are presented in a language resembling C#) might then look like:

```
Boolean GetSamples(ulong[] samples, ulong[] features){
    // assume features and hashes fit in ulong
    // return true if no features
    Boolean first = true; // no features yet
    int n = samples.Length();
    ulong[] hashes = new ulong[n]; // min in slot
    foreach (ulong f in features) {
        for (int i = 0; i < n; i++) {
            ulong hash = Hash(f, i);
            // see if hash is smallest
            if (first || hash < hashes[i]) {
                hashes[i] = hash;
                samples[i] = f;
            }
        }
        first = false;
    }
    return first;
}
```

where Hash takes in a feature and a sample number, and returns a reproducible pseudo-random value.

We measure the cost of computing in the number of bits of pseudo-randomness needed per feature per selection. By this measure, a single selection function would come out quite well, with cost inversely proportional to the number of samples (and constant per feature). We seek to obtain comparable cost even when picking multiple values using multiple functions.

The pseudo-code above does not achieve this: the cost is constant at one evaluation per feature per sample. Naively, our goal seems impossible: even if our features are drawn from some finite pool, each sample would seem to require the evaluation of a pseudo-random mapping to a range as large as the pool, to guarantee that the mapping is one-to-one, as required to ensure the well-definedness of sampling. This leads to a pseudo-randomness budget equal to the logarithm of the size of the feature pool.

However, while complete evaluation would require this much work, partial evaluation and clever choice of functions can do better. We need not fully evaluate our pseudo-random function, once we know enough to know that some other value is smaller, proving that this value, if fully evaluated, will not be smallest. For Alta Vista, we chose to divide each of our functions into two pieces: a one-byte piece which we could evaluate in parallel for multiple functions by dividing a large function value into bytes, used for the most-significant portion of a set of mappings, and a one-to-one function used to break ties at the byte level, evaluated only when the first byte was among the smallest in its slot. The number of evaluations of our large one-to-one function is thereby reduced by a factor of roughly 256, which was a considerable saving, reducing the number of computers needed to rebuild the index at Alta Vista by roughly that factor.

If full evaluations produce 64 bits of value, while the prefix uses only eight bits, the number of 8-bit values we generate is reduced (per output value) to $\frac{264}{256} = \frac{65}{64}$: one for the prefix, and (in the limit, as documents get long) one time in 256 we generate eight more bytes to break ties.

This choice of lengths was sufficient for the Alta Vista corpus, but runs a little short for today's corpora. Google, at last report, indexes at least 50 billion documents, which is approximately 25 times 2 to the 31st power. This places the square of the corpus size above the largest 64 bit integer, making hash collisions quite likely; with current corpora, we would recommend using at least 96 bit hash values.

Note that, at the cost of increasing the number of ties, we could have economized the expected number of bits slightly, by noticing that with a four-bit prefix we can compute twice as many prefixes in the same number of bits. We would increase the rate of collision to 1 in 16, but $\frac{1}{2} + \frac{8}{16} = 1 < \frac{65}{64}$, which is slightly smaller (one-half, because we can generate two prefixes in each byte; eight-sixteenths, because one time in 16 we need 8 more bytes). We implemented this, only to discover that our document lengths actually caused this to be less efficient in practice: at eight bits, in a few slots there was often only one winner (and so we could skip the evaluation of the extra bits), but there were almost always multiple winners when the prefix was only four bits. Moreover, too much buffer space is needed to store candidate winners for everything to fit comfortably in a first-level cache. Consequently, we kept things at eight bits of prefix, despite the slight theoretical asymptotic superiority of four.

We need a small subroutine `ResolveBuf` to keep the number of retained samples bounded, which we will present in more detail following the sampling code, which looks something like:

```
Boolean GetSamples(ulong[] samples, Features features){
    const int BUFLEN=16; // buffered feature storage
    Boolean first = true; // are we starting up?
    int n = samples.Length();
    int prefixn = (n+7)/8; // 8 bytes in 64-bit hash
    ubyte[] minprefix = new ubyte[n]; // winner by slot
    ulong[,] buf = new ulong[n, BUFLEN];
    // all features in buf[j, ..] produce minprefix[j]
    int nInBuf = new int[n]; // number of contenders
```

```
foreach (ulong f in features) {
    for (int i = 0; i < prefixn; i++) {
        ulong prefhash = HashP(f, i);
        for (int j=0; j < 8; j++, prefhash >>= 8) {
            int index = 8*i + j;
            if (index < n &&
                    (first || prefhash & 0xff <=
                            minprefix[index])) {
                if (first || prefhash & 0xff <
                                minprefix[index]) {
                    nInBuf[index] = 0;
                    minprefix[n] = prefhash & 0xff;
                }
                if (nInBuf[index] == BUFLEN)
                    resolveBuf(nInBuf, buf, index);
                buf[index, nInBuf[index]++] = f;
            }
        }
    }
    first = FALSE;

                if (!first) {
                    for (int i = 0; i < n; i++) {
                        if (nInBuf[i] > 1)
                            ResolveBuf(nInBuf, buf, i);
                        samples[i] = buf[i, 0];
                    }
                }
                return first;
            }
```

In the above, ResolveBuf examines all the elements of the specified buffer, computes the low-order values for the specified index, and all values in buf, places the best in the first spot, and resets nInBuf to 1, as below:

```
void ResolveBuf(int[] n, ulong[,] buf, int j) {
  // with candidate minima for function j stored
  // in buf[j,0], …, buf[j,n[j]-1]], select one with
  // smallest tail hash, and reduce n[j] to 1.
    if (n[j] <= 1) return;
  // Don't need to pick a winner
    ulong hash0 = HashT(buf[j,0], j); // Get final bits
      for (int i = 1; i < n[j]; i++) {
        ulong hash_i = HashT(buf[j,i], j);
        if (hash_i < hash0) {
            buf[j,0] = buf[j,i];
            hash0 = hash_i;
        }
      }
    n[j] = 1;
}
```

HashP and HashT are the prefix and tail hash functions, seeded using the feature and slot index. Note that we rely on HashT to guarantee that values are distinct (otherwise there is no single pre-image for the minimal hash). Note further that we expect in these code fragments that the features are distinct; if the input features may contain duplicates, it would be wise to add a quick check when adding something to the buffer that it is not already present, or else the buffer may fill with duplicate features. The current code remains correct either way, but if large numbers of duplicates are expected, it would be better to fix GetSamples to check if feature f is already present in buf before trying to insert it; for small buffer sizes, probing is fast enough. For larger-sized buffers, we are quite fond of Pagh and Rodler's cuckoo hashing (although not really in the scope of this volume), which can be expected to operate efficiently at nearly-full capacity, when used with multiple probes.

3.3 RABIN HASHING REVISITED

The hash functions used at Alta Vista were Rabin permutations, alluded to in Section 2.2.

Rabin recognized some additional algebraic properties of his earlier work on hashing with Karp that could be gained by working over polynomial rings instead of integers modulo a prime, although modular arithmetic has some simplicity advantages.

In this section, we examine more precisely how to implement such permutations efficiently, and how to slide such a permutation along a fixed-size window on an input block.

In what follows, we consider only Rabin hash functions defined in $GF(2^{64})$, the Galois field with 2^{64} elements (including zero). We can view elements of the field as 64-bit unsigned integers representing polynomials in $GF(2)[x]$. For some practical reasons, we represent the x^{63} coefficient in the lowest-order (1's) bit of the integer, and the x^0 coefficient in the high-order bit; by doing this, on a little-endian architecture (such as an X86), viewing a string as a polynomial, the representation of one character followed by nulls has the same numerical value when read as a byte, a 16-bit word, a 32-bit word, or a 64-bit word. We can thus efficiently read the largest possible matching unit of the string, when working in less-principled languages than C#, such as the K&R C in which we first developed early version of this code for Alta Vista.

Addition in the field is exclusive-or of the integers, but we will need to pick a specific representation of the field in order to define multiplication.

To do so, we randomly select a primitive polynomial p of degree 64, with Boolean coefficients. Galois theory informs us that $GF(2)[x]/(p) \cong GF(2^{64})$, that is, the ring of Boolean polynomials modulo p is isomorphic to the Galois field we seek, where elements of the field can be taken to be the class of polynomials which differ by multiples of p. We can represent $p - x^{64}$ as a 64-bit unsigned integer q, remembering that we store the high-degree terms of the polynomial in the low-order bits of the integer.

We construct a table `bybyte[8, 256]`, so that `bybyte[a, n]` $= n * x^{8a+8} (\bmod\ p)$, viewing the product as a polynomial; $8a + 8$ reflects that we append 8 zeros after the string; the multiplicative factor of 8 reflects that we perform this computation one byte at a time, not one bit. For example, `bybyte[0, 0X80]` $= q$, since 2^{64} encodes the polynomial x^{64}, and $q = p - x^{64}$. Thus, $x^{64} (\bmod\ p) = -q = q$ (because our field has characteristic two, so every value is its own additive complement). We complete the spine of `bybyte` by noticing the following.

1. Multiplication by x corresponds to a logical shift by 1 (to the right, since we store our polynomial with the high-degree term at the right).

2. A bit shift by one place produces an x^{64} term exactly when the low-order bit is one.

3. Adding p to a degree 64 polynomial produces a polynomial of degree at most 63, whose representation as an integer fits in a 64-bit unsigned location.

Consequently, we can fill in `bybyte[b,j]` for power of 2 values of j by setting `bybyte[0, 0x80]` to q, and noting that `bybyte[b, j >> 1]` = `bybyte[b,j]` $*x (\bmod\ p)$, and `bybyte[b+1, 0x80]` = `bybyte[b, 1]` $*x (\bmod p)$; linearity fills in the rest of the array, as in the code below.

To define a permutation of 64-bit non-negative integers, we map j to the canonical representative of the equivalence class of the polynomial with coefficients of a leading 1 followed by the bits of j followed by 64 zeros. We prepend a leading 1 so that the value zero becomes non-zero; we affix 64 more zeros so that consecutive values become spaced far apart, making the output more random-appearing:

```
public class Hash64 {

    public ulong Empty; // hash of empty string
    private ulong[] poly; // xor by 0 or q
    private const ulong One = ((ulong) 1) << 63;
    private const ulong Ex = ((ulong 1)) << 62;

    Hash64(ulong q) { // constructor
        // x^64 + q should be a primitive polynomial
        Empty = q;
        poly = new ulong[]{0, q};
    }

    private ulong mulX(ulong a) {
        return (a >> 1) ^ poly[a & 1];
    }

    private ulong mul(ulong a, ulong b){
        ulong res = 0L;
        while (b != 0){
            if ((b & One) != 0)
                res ^= a;
            a = mulX(a);
            b <<= 1;
        }
        return res;
    }
}
```

```
public ulong Extend(ulong f, byte[] s, int len) {
    // slow, but obviously correct
    for (int i = 0; i < len; i++){
        f ^= s[i];
        for (int j = 0; j < 8; j++)
            f = mulX(f);
    }
    return f;
}


public ulong Hash(byte[] s, int len) {
// Extend x^64, a leading 1
    return Extend(Empty, s, len);
}
}
```

A few utility procedures and constants are included above. One and Ex represent the polynomials 1 and x. MulX multiplies a polynomial by x, increasing the degree of the polynomial by one, subtracting out the modulus when the multiplication would cause the degree to equal 64.

Mul multiplies two polynomials modulo our special polynomial.

The poly array allows us to avoid a branch; the array obviates the statement:

```
private ulong mulX(ulong a) {
    if ((a & 1) == 1)
        return (a >> 1) ^ Empty;
    else
        return a >> 1;
}
```

which would cause a branch misprediction half of the time, in all those places where the (missing) sixty-fourth bit might be set, such as in mulX. A cached memory lookup is faster than breaking the instruction pipeline on most processors.

Further, by using a byte-indexed array, we can avoid the inner for loop on j by precomputing the impact of a byte being shifted by 8 bits, resulting in the following code for Extend:

```
    private ulong[] bybyte;

    private ulong mulXIf(ulong a, ulong x) {
        return ((x & 1) == 0)? a : mulX(a);
    }


Hash64(ulong q) {
    ... // as above, plus
        bybyte = new ulong[256];
        bybyte[0] = 0;
        ulong f = Empty;
// 0x80 shifted right 8 places would put
// a 1 in the first non-existent position
// yielding Empty after XOR
        for (int i = 0x80; i != 0; i >>= 1) (
            bybyte[i] = f;
            f = mulX(f);
        }
        for (int i = 2; i < by.Length; i <<= 1)
            for (int j = 1; j < i; j++)
                bybyte[i^j] = bybyte[i] ^ bybyte[j];
        }
    }


    public ulong Extend(ulong f, byte[] s, int len) {
        for (int i = 0; i < len; i++)
            f = (f >> 8) ^ bybyte[(f ^ s[i]) & 0xff];
        return f;
    }
```

Note that we initialize bybyte[0] to 0, reflecting that no overflow results from a leading byte of 0. We initialize position 0x80 to Empty because shifting by eight bits moves x^{56} to x^{64}, congruent to Empty (i.e., q) modulo $x^{64} + q$. To initialize the other power of two entries, we note that they correspond to a single bit, so we multiply the previous value by x, by shifting and reducing. The remaining positions are then computed using linearity, adding previously computed positions.

We can further extend the `bybyte` table to two dimensions, to shift by 1 up to 8 bytes, eliminating the data-dependency on shifts of `f`, and allowing us to instead write the following code:

```
public class Hash64 {
    ...
    private ulong[,] bybyte;

    private void InitByByte(ref ulong[,] by, ulong f) {
        by = new ulong[8, 256];
        for (int b = 0; b < by.GetLength(0); b++) {
            by[b, 0] = 0;
            for (int i = 0x80; i != 0; i >>= 1) {
                by[b, i] = f;
                f = mulX(f);
            }
            for (int i = 2; i < by.GetLength(1); i <<= 1)
                for (int j = 1; j < i; j++)
                    by[b, i ^ j] = by[b, i] ^ by[b, j];
        }
    }

    Hash64(ulong q) {
        ...
        InitByByte(ref bybyte, q);
    }
```

```
public ulong Extend(ulong f, byte[] s, int len) {
    int i = 0;
    while (len >= 8) {
      f =   bybyte[7, (s[i] ^ f) & 0xff] ^
            bybyte[6, ((s[i+1] ^ f) >> 8) & 0xff] ^
            bybyte[5, ((s[i+2] ^ f) >> 16) & 0xff] ^
            bybyte[4, ((s[i+3] ^ f) >> 24) & 0xff] ^
            bybyte[3, ((s[i+4] ^ f) >> 32) & 0xff] ^
            bybyte[2, ((s[i+5] ^ f) >> 40) & 0xff] ^
            bybyte[1, ((s[i+6] ^ f) >> 48) & 0xff] ^
            bybyte[0, ((s[i+7] ^ f) >> 56) & 0xff];
      i += 8;
      len -= 8;
    }
    while (len-- > 0)
      f = (f >> 8) ^ bybyte[0, (f ^ s[i++]) & 0xff];
    return f;

  }

}
```

In the version of Extend above, the first loop handles most of the byte array, leaving only a tail of length less than eight for the clean-up loop at the end. If we are fingerprinting objects of size equal to a fingerprint, we can produce the slightly simpler:

```
public class Hash64 {
    ...
    public ulong Extend(ulong f, ulong[] s, int len) {
        int i = 0;
        while (len-- > 0) {
            f ^= s[i++];
            f =  bybyte[7,  f & 0xff] ^
                 bybyte[6, (f >> 8)  & 0xff] ^
                 bybyte[5, (f >> 16) & 0xff] ^
                 bybyte[4, (f >> 24) & 0xff] ^
                 bybyte[3, (f >> 32) & 0xff] ^
                 bybyte[2, (f >> 40) & 0xff] ^
                 bybyte[1, (f >> 48) & 0xff] ^
                 bybyte[0, (f >> 56) & 0xff];
        }
        return f;
    }
```

We can turn the final `while` loop to deal with misalignment into a fall-through `switch` statement using Duff's device, at the cost of forcing an ordering on the `bybyte` lookups; if we did this, we could replace the index arithmetic with increments to access the input array. Duff's device, for those unfamiliar with it, is a particularly nasty perversion of the C language, wrapping a loop around a `switch` statement so that the first time through the loop, a subset of the unrolled loop is executed, and the entire unrolling is executed later.

Rabin hashes, being algebraically simple, are amenable to a few further mathematical tricks. We can compute the hash of the concatenation of two strings, knowing only the hashes of the two strings and the length of the second. As polynomials, we need to recognize that hashing is linear: `hash(a^b)=hash(a)^hash(b)`, and `hash($x^j$*a)=hash($x^j$)*hash(a)`, once we compensate for the leading one bit, which otherwise is cancelled when adding two strings. More precisely, for strings of the same length, `hash(a^b)=hash(a)^hash(b)^hash($x^{len(a)}$)`, a distinction we conveniently ignore in the rest of this paragraph, but which shows up in the discussion and code that follow. Using this, we conclude that `hash(concat(a, b))` = `hash(a*$x^{len(b)}$)` `^ hash(b)` = `hash( $x^{len(b)}$)` `* hash(a)` `^hash(b)`. We build a table of the binary powers of x, and use linearity to construct the hash of arbitrary powers, using school-boy multiplication, as exhibited below, after adding an array of powers of x (and a short array of zeros to skip the multiplication for small powers, using `Extend` instead):

```
    private byte[] zeros;  // of size ZEROBLOCK
    private ulong[] powers; // x^(8*2^i) mod p
    const int LOGZEROBLOCK = 8;
    const int ZEROBLOCK = 1 << LOGZEROBLOCK;


Hash64(ulong q) {
    ...
    zeros =  new byte[ZEROBLOCK];
    zeros.Initialize();
    powers = new ulong[64];
    powers[0] = 1L << 55; // x^8, length is in bytes
    ulong el = 1; // 2^(i+1)
    for (int i = 1; i < powers.Length; i++, el <<= 1)
        powers[i] = Concat(powers[i - 1] ^ q, 0, l);
}
```

Having created and initialized the powers of x and a small array of zeros, we are ready to write `Concat`, remembering that we need to eliminate the one bit leading the affixed fingerprint, and shift the prefixed fingerprint by some combination of direct extension by zeros, so that the remaining length is divisible by 256, or by multiplication by an appropriate power of two.

On the following page, as a second extension, we note that we often compute hashes of a sliding window of fixed-length, advancing by individual bytes, or by words. To facilitate this, we note that a sliding window of a fixed length in bytes can have individual phrase hashes computed without recomputing *ab initio* by observing that `(hash(ds)*x)^hash(1d1*`x^l`)+hash(a)=hash(sa)`, where `ds` is the concatenation of `d` and `textsfs`, and `1d1` refers to adding a leading 1 to `d` and flipping the low-order bit to introduce the leading 1 for `sa`, where l is the bit-length of `s`. We introduce new `spanbyte` tables to facilitate the computation of the shifted hashes, as below, modifying slightly to assume that `d` and `a` are `ulong`-sized, instead of single bytes, so that we need no intermediate shifting. The `spanbyte` tables are computed so as to eliminate bytes shifted by the bit length of s:

```
public ulong Concat(ulong ha, ulong hb, ulong blen) {
  // ha is Hash(s), hb is Hash(t), and blen is
  // t.Length. Produce Hash(s+t)
        ha ^= Empty;
        // hb is a fingerprint, so has a leading 1 in its
```

```
        // polynomial. Wipe it with an extra 1 at end of
        // ha, shifted by one bit, which kills a p
        int i;
        ulong x = blen;
        // Knock off low-order bits by extension
        int low = ((int) x) & (ZEROBLOCK - 1);
        if (low != 0)
            ha = Extend(ha, zeros, low);
        x >>= LOGZEROBLOCK;
        i = LOGZEROBLOCK;  // already did these.
        // Do remainder by schoolboy multiplication,
        // modifying multiplier as we go using powers
        while (x != 0) {
            if ((x & 1) != 0) {
                ulong m = 0;
                ulong bit;
                ulong e = powers[i];
                for (bit = ((ulong)1) << 63;
                     bit != 0; bit >>= 1) {
                    if ((e & bit) != 0)
                        m ^= ha;
                    ha = mulX(ha);
                }
                ha = m;
            }
            x >>= 1;
            i++;
        }

        // having opened room in ha for blen new bytes, and
        // and having compensated for the leading 1 in hb,
        // and shifted by blen*8+64, xor in hb
        return ha ^ hb;
    }
```

To incorporate sliding window hash computations for a fixed size window of **span** bytes, add the following, assuming that **span** is divisible by 8:

```
public class Hash64 {
    ...
      private ulong[,] spanbybyte;

      Hash64(ulong q, int span) {
          ...
          spanbybyte = new byte[8,256];
          ulong qs = Concat(Empty, 0, span);
      }

    public ulong Slide(ulong f, ulong d, ulong a) {
      // f = h(d+s), result = h(s+a), s has length span-1
      // kill old leading 1 (one bit before d), and add
      // next leading 1 (at end of d, so one bit before s
        d ^= p ^ (((uint) 1) << 63);
          f ^= spanbybyte[7, d & 0xff] ^
              spanbybyte[6, (d >> 8)  & 0xff] ^
              spanbybyte[5, (d >> 16) & 0xff] ^
              spanbybyte[4, (d >> 24) & 0xff] ^
              spanbybyte[3, (d >> 32) & 0xff] ^
              spanbybyte[2, (d >> 40) & 0xff] ^
              spanbybyte[1, (d >> 48) & 0xff] ^
              spanbybyte[0, d >> 56];


          // f is now h(s), so extend by a
          f ^= a;
          f = bybyte[7, f & 0xff] ^
              bybyte[6, (f >> 8)  & 0xff] ^
              bybyte[5, (f >> 16) & 0xff] ^
              bybyte[4, (f >> 24) & 0xff] ^
              bybyte[3, (f >> 32) & 0xff] ^
              bybyte[2, (f >> 40) & 0xff] ^
              bybyte[1, (f >> 48) & 0xff] ^
              bybyte[0, f >> 56];
          return f;

    }
}
```

To make all of this work, we must have a way to generate random primitive polynomials of the desired degree. To do this, we need a very small amount of group theory.

A *group* is a set with an associative multiplication operator, a multiplicative identity element (1), and an inverse operator, so that for any x in the group $x \cdot x^{-1} = x^{-1} \cdot x = 1$.

Given an element x, the *ideal* generated by x, (x) is the set of powers of x. The set of non-zero polynomials of degree less than k with coefficients in $\{0, 1\}$ has size $2^k - 1$: all of the binary strings of length k except for the string of all zeros. Given any degree k polynomial p with a one for its constant term, x is invertible modulo p: for some q, $p = qx + 1$. Taking $x^{-1} = q$, $x^{-1}x = qx = p - 1 \equiv p + 1 \equiv 1$, because using the Booleans as coefficients for polynomials means that addition and subtraction are equivalent. Any power of x has the corresponding power of x^{-1} as an inverse, so the set of powers of x modulo p forms a group. Because the number of Boolean polynomials of degree less than k is finite, this field is finite. By the pigeonhole principle, there are two different powers of x, x^j, and x^k which are equal to one another, with $0 \leq k < j$. But then, by the usual rules of exponents, $x^{j-k} \equiv x^j x^{k^{-1}} \equiv x^j x^{j^{-1}} \equiv 1$. Hence, there is a least positive power of x congruent to 1. Call this the *order* of x modulo p. This is also equal to the number of distinct powers of x modulo p, since the next power multiplies $1 \cdot x \equiv x$, which is where we started. As seen above, any collision of powers leads to a power producing 1 with exponent less than the larger. Consequently, the number of distinct powers is also equal to the order of x modulo p.

Because of this, we can also describe the number of distinct powers as the order of the ideal. In searching for primitive polynomials, we are searching for p of degree k such that the order of x is $2^k - 1$. We will guarantee this by picking random polynomials of the desired order with non-zero constant term, and testing.

If a polynomial is primitive, $x^{2^k} \equiv x^{2^k - 1}x \equiv x$, because the order of x would be $2^k - 1$. This would be the first exponent to produce 1. But it is easy to check if $x^{2^k} \equiv x$, if we have the ability to square one polynomial modulo another: If squaring x and its powers k times. fails to result in x, we have chosen poorly, and choose a new random p.

Sadly, getting the desired result is no guarantee (these polynomials are the equivalent of Carmichael numbers in the integers, ones where pseudo-primality testing is inadequate): if $j | 2^k - 1$ and $x^j \equiv 1$, any multiple of j is an exponent producing a one. We can check that this doesn't happen with a few exponentiations: $2^k - 1$ has a small fixed set of positive divisors, and we can verify that none of them produce a unit result, given the ability to raise a polynomial to an arbitrary positive power, which we can do by combining squaring and multiplication by x, as follows in the code below. We can precompute the prime divisors of $2^k - 1$ and raise x to the succession of all but one divisor in turn to guarantee that none of them results in 1. Since we have verified that the order of x is a divisor of $2^k - 1$, by raising x to all maximal proper divisors of $2^k - 1$ we can be sure that when none of these are multiples of the order, thereby establishing that the order is in fact $2^k - 1$.

Given the number of primitive polynomials, generating and testing random polynomials should often find a primitive polynomial (for degree 64) after a few dozen tests; the fraction of primitive polynomials is easily shown to be at least one in k. By listing the prime factors of $2^{64} - 1$ in an array, powers, we can use repeated calls to pow to exclude an individual factor, to verify that we do not produce a one too early.

We write it this way (instead of computing the product) so that we can switch to larger degree (for a while) without using bignums. The factors of all $2^{8k} - 1$ fit in a ulong until $8k = 184$, where the largest factor is an algebraic factor, a degree coming from the cyclotomic polynomial of degree 88 arising in the factorization of $x^{184} - 1$. The largest factor of $2^{184} - 1$ takes 88 bits to encode, too large for a long integer. From there, the next value of $8k$, 192, has a factor exactly equal to $2^{64} - 1$, which is only a problem when using signed 64 bit integers for the factors. This is an algebraic factor, since $2^{192} - 1$ is a difference of cubes. At $2^{208} - 1$, we get a 96-bit cyclotomic algebraic factor, observed by viewing the whole as a difference of eighth powers, so the factors again do not fit.

If we allow ourselves to take slightly smaller fields, the factorizations of $2^{182} - 1$, $2^{190} - 1$, and $2^{207} - 1$ present no 64-bit obstacles. Moreover, all cyclotomic polynomials are quite regular, so we could encode the prime cyclotomic factors algorithmically without straining the range of long integers. Or we could satisfy ourselves with primitive polynomials only of degrees leading to easily factored sizes, thus skipping degree 184 and 208, substituting degrees 192 and 216, or we could resign ourselves to using bignums, and accept the associated loss in performance.

In testing polynomials, we should choose randomly among polynomials which include a non-zero unit term. Polynomials without unit are divisible by x, so not irreducible, so the residues cannot form a field (except for the trivial case of the polynomial x). Suppose that our polynomial $p = xq$, producing a primitive multiplicative group from the powers of x. In that case, for some least j, $x^j \equiv q$, but then $x^{j+1} \equiv xq \equiv 0$. All larger powers of x will still multiply out to zero, so we can never find a power that generates 1, showing that the elements do not form a group.

Among those polynomials not divisible by x of degree k, a little group theory which is beyond the ambitions of this book tells us that the number of primitive polynomials is $\frac{\Phi(n)}{n-1}$, where $\Phi(n)$ is Euler's totient function, the number of whole numbers relatively prime to n:

```
public class Hash64 {
    ...
    public ulong pow(ulong power) { // Ex^^power
        if (power < 64) return (One >> (int)power);
        ulong res = pow(power >> 1);
        return mulXIf(mul(res, res), power);
    }
}
```

```
public ulong pow(ulong n, ulong power) { // n^^power
    if (power <= 1) return (power == 0) ? One : n;
    ulong res = pow(mul(n,n), power >> 1);
    if ((power & 1) != 0) res = mul(res, n);
    return res;
}

private ulong pow(ulong[] powers, int start, int omit){
    if (start >= (powers.Length - 1))
      return (omit == start) ? Ex : pow(powers[start]);
    ulong res = pow(powers, start+1, omit);
    if (start != omit) res = pow(res, powers[start]);
    return res;
}

private ulong pow(ulong[] powers, int omit) {
// Ex^powers[0]*…*powers[omit-1]*powers[omit+1]*…)
    return pow(powers, 0, omit);
}

static private ulong[] factors =
      new ulong[]{3,5,17,257,641,65537,6700417};

public Boolean IsPrimitive(ulong p) {
    for (int i = 0; i < factors.Length; i++) {
      ulong prod = pow(factors, i);
      if ((prod == One) ||
          (pow(prod, factors[i]) != One))
            return FALSE;
    }
    return TRUE;
}
}
```

CHAPTER 4

Uniform Sampling after Alta Vista

In the 15 years since we worked on Alta Vista (while applying these techniques to Bing, and subsequently), we have discovered a few ways to compute consistent random samples from streams, typically using fewer random bits. In this chapter, we consider some of these approaches, delivering improvements from a factor of four to a factor of roughly 20, as the sections of this chapter will present. Such improvements are valuable, since the indexed size of the web has grown from tens of millions of pages to tens of billions in the intervening years.

4.1 USING LESS RANDOMNESS TO IMPROVE SAMPLING EFFICIENCY

Restricting our attention to finite pools of features, as in the code samples above, we are no longer constrained by well-orderedness, just by total orderings and one-to-oneness of valuation mappings. Instead of picking fixed size integers, imagine that our functions map to binary expansions of values between zero and one of arbitrary precision (that is, proper fractions of arbitrarily-long integers divided by arbitrary powers of two), using some easily seeded pseudo-random process to generate bits. To guarantee that the map is one-to-one, suppose that, after some predetermined (but unspecified and henceforth ignored) large number of bits, we output the input value (but we delay this as long as we reasonably can, because the input features are probably not particularly random).

To avoid generating so many bits, we can examine the bits as we generate them to determine which value is smallest as the fractional part of a binary number. As long as two values have the same expansion and are contending to be smallest, continue to produce bits. When the values diverge, prefer the value with a zero instead of a one. If the values are uniformly random, we expect that zeros and ones are equally likely, so two values can be expected to diverge after examining two bits—half the time, the first bits will differ, a quarter of the time the first bits will match but the second bits will differ, an eighth of the time the first two will match but the third will differ, and so on. Remember the smallest and its expansion, and compare new values to that, changing the remembered value when new values prove to be still smaller.

To better take advantage of this, pick an easily seeded pseudo-random number generator, such as RC4. We don't need the cryptographic benefits of RC4, but we do want something which can generate a very large set of seemingly random and independent bitstreams; the pseudo-random number generators in most C# libraries have a set of seed values which is too small for our purposes. Suppose that we are trying to produce samples 1 through n, given features $\{f_i\}$, and we have seedable bitstream generators b_s, where s is the seed. We choose seeds (f_i, k) for natural number values of k. For non-zero values of k, we could take our value to be generated by this stream, but that would require reseeding our generator for every input value and sample position to determine if it might be smallest. To increase the efficiency of this process, just as Alta Vista used a stream to produce only the high-order bits of the value stream, we derive the most-significant bits for all k from the stream b_0, as explained below. We invoke the other generators only to resolve ties.

If all we cared about was minimizing seedings (holding it to one per input feature), we could just interleave all of our values into a single stream, constructing countably many streams from one stream by placing the values in a two-dimensional matrix, and enumerating terms along diagonals. This would require us to evaluate our stream to a great length to get the first few bits for larger values of k, and we might find ourselves needing enough bits to exhaust all entropy in the seed. To avoid this, and the need for continual reseeding, we use the stream generated by b_0 to produce the first few bits of all streams, and (while we hope rarely to need to do this) we use b_k for later bits, when the leading bits result in a tie. The values of the bits to be produced must be independent of the existence of any ties, in order to preserve the consistency of selection.

To produce uniform leading bits more efficiently while trying to find the lexicographically largest, we take consecutive bits until we reach a bit with the value one. We expect to examine two random bits in order to find our first one bit. We expect that, with n different inputs to consider, that the longest sequence of zeros before finding a one has length roughly $\log_2 n$, and that the probability of finding that two among all our inputs result in the same longest sequence of zeros both followed by a one is at most one-half: if two inputs produce identical initial sequences of zeros, half the time the next bit should separate them. By maintaining a small pool of candidate winners, we can delay producing the bits which follow the first one bit, in the hope that some subsequent input will produce an even-longer initial sequence of zeros. When we reach the end of an input stream, we need to take the winning pre-image (if unique), or determine a winner by considering the trailing bitstreams, waiting for the bitstreams to diverge, and preferring the input which produces a zero at the point of divergence. If the buffer is completely full when a new candidate is found, we need to perform the same winner-determination as at the end of input, leaving only the winning-so-far input in the buffer, just as in `ResolveBuf` above.

If the set of candidate values contains duplicates, we need to check to see if a candidate is already present in the buffer: no amount of extension by random bits will separate identical candidates.

To implement this, we modify the previous program. First, we need a way to manage a stream of randomness to extract the number of leading zeros:

```
class RandomBits {
    int bitsLeft = 0;
    ulong randomLeft = 0;
    private Random r;
    RandomBits(Random f) {
        r = f;
    }
    public int NextRun() { // length of zeros at start
        int res = 0;
        Boolean done = FALSE;
        while (randomLeft == 0) {
            res += bitsLeft;
            randomLeft = r.Next();
            bitsLeft = 64; // whatever r.Next produces
        }
        do { // randomLeft != 0, needn't check bitsLeft
            done = (randomLeft & 1) != 0;
            randomLeft >>>= 1;
            bitsLeft--; // byte-at-a-time with lookup
            res++;      // table might be better
        } while (!done);
    return res;
    }
}
```

This code should not be used verbatim; the Random class in C# which we purport to employ in the above uses 32-bit seeds, and produces 31 bits of value on a call to Next; this gives us a space which would have been too small even for the corpus in Alta Vista. But the class we want is approximately the Random class, if only it were suitably extended; for realistic-sized corpora, we would much prefer seed sizes of at least 64 bits, if not longer, and we would prefer integral values which were simple unsigned values.

For a buffer of size m, we expect to exceed the buffer with probability at most $\frac{1}{2^m}$: any input which matches the best sequence so far resets the buffer with probability one-half, and expands the set of buffered items with the same probability. Consequently, a 32-entry buffer should rarely prove insufficient; as a result, the expected amount of work to determine the winning input item is the cost of producing two expected bits of pseudorandomness from bitstream 0, plus the expected value of producing the low-order bits for the expected-to-be-small number of inputs in the buffer.

One might hope to improve the performance of RandomBits.Next slightly by using a lookup table on the low-order byte, or by (at least) skipping over zero bytes. This is unlikely to help much: again, the expected return value is only two, so the low-order byte will most often be non-zero:

```
Boolean GetSamples(ulong[] result, features) {
    int nsamples=result.Length();
    feature[,] buf = new feature[nsamples, BUFLEN];
    int[] prefix = new int[nsamples];
    int[] nInBuf= new int[nsamples];
    Boolean first = true;
    foreach (feature f in features) {
        RandomBits r = new RandomBits(new Random(f));
        for (int i = 0; i < nsamples; i++) {
            int log = r.NextRun();
            if (first || log >= prefix[i]) {
                if (first || log > prefix[i]) {
                    nInBuf[i] = 0;
                    prefix[i] = log;
                }
                if (nInBuf[i] == BUFLEN)
                    ResolveBuf(nInBuf, buf, i);
                buf[i, nInBuf[i]++] = f;
            }
        }
    }
    first = false;
    if (!first)
        for (int i = 0; i < NSAMPLES; i++) {
            if (nInBuf[i] > 1)
                ResolveBuf(nInBuf, buf, i);
            result[i] = buf[0][i];
        }
    return first;
}
```

To further reduce the cost of these low-order bits (and to reduce the number of times the pseudo-random generator needs to be seeded), we could produce a few bits after the first one, but this would increase the expected cost to at least three bits per input per selection, instead of just over two. For some input lengths and desired number of selections, and for a given seeding cost, this might still win.

As before, `ResolveBuf` is meant to reduce the buffer size to one, picking more bits to break ties. Since we already have a two-bit generator, we can implement this by allocating new `RandomBits` generators using the feature `f` and the index `i` as seed; we can keep a small buffer of these generators in order to resolve ties that need multiple choices:

```
void ResolveBuf(int[] n, ulong[,] buf, int j) {
    int nn = n[j];
    if (nn <= 1) return; // Don't need to pick a winner
// buf[j, 0..nn-1] contain features which are tied
    RandomBits[] rbits = new RandomBits[BUFLEN];
    for (int i = 0; i < nn; i++)
// any way of producing a pairing here would suffice
        rbits[j] = new RandomBits(
            buf[j, i] + "**sample number**" + j);
// each pass through the next part should cut nn
// down to expected two, and half the time one.
    while (nn > 1) {
        int nnNext = 1;
        int hash_0 = rbits[0].Next();
        for (int i = 1; i < nn; i++) {
            int hash_i = rbits[i].Next();
            if (hash_i >= hash_0) {
                if (hash_i > hash_0) {
                    // new outright winner
                    hash_0 = hash_i;
                    nnNext = 0;
                }
                rbits[nnNext] = rbits[i];
                buf[j,nnNext++] = buf[j,i];
                // done with slot i
            }
        }
        nn = nnNext;
    }
    n[j] = 1;
}
```

I conjectured that this four-fold reduction, to two expected bits per sample, might be optimal: that any uniform consistent sampling approach with replacement had to consume at least two bits of pseudorandomness per input per sample.

4.2   CONJECTURES VS. THEOREMS

As might be supposed from the section title, I was mistaken (in this case, hiding behind *we* would be an injustice to my co-authors, who labored under no such misapprehension). For sufficiently long input streams, and sufficiently large numbers of desired samples, we can do better. We will specify some examples of sufficiently large numbers, and present counterexamples, and an improved method of sampling.

When applying sampling to web pages, and planning to apply supershingling, some observed data about web pages is helpful: typical web pages are roughly 1,000 words long. Supershingling works well, for the usual range of desirable thresholds, using between 32 and 128 samples. For concreteness, let's suppose 1,024 words and 128 samples.

With 1,024 words leading to 1,024 features, the probability that any given input feature results in the smallest image is 1 in 2 to the 10th. The probability that a given feature is selected for any sample is under one-eighth (if features were chosen without repetition, one-eighth would be right; since we allow repetition, it is slightly lower). If we could find an unbiased consistent way to rapidly reject a feature from consideration as being chosen for any sample, we might hope to need many fewer bits than the expected 256 bits resulting from an expected two bits chosen for 128 samples.

One such way would be to find a way to bias the first bits of randomness in our selection algorithm. Suppose that we used the scheme defined above, but the first bit was much more likely to be a one than a zero. If, for instance, the bits were ten times as likely to be a one, then rather than needing to examine roughly two bits until we found a one, we would need to examine a single bit nine times out of ten, and an expected two bits one time in ten, leading to an expected consumption of only 1.2 bits of randomness per input per selection, with a few small caveats.

First, we do not know how to produce such a stream efficiently at the bit level. But this is all just a *gedankenexperiment* so far; the next few paragraphs describe a practical realization of this approach, and reduce the costs even more.

Second, there is now some chance that all inputs, for some sample, produce a leading one. This breaks the arguments above about a bounded buffer being sufficient (although we can deal with this: do not remember all the input values producing a leading one, remember only that no input has produced a leading zero yet, and run the input stream through the low-order bit generator to find a point of divergence), but it changes the probability of needing to use the low-order bits. If the bias is sufficiently small, and the documents are sufficiently long, this happens rarely enough that the costs are supportable, but it can and will happen sometimes. Fortunately, it does not happen too often: for a given sample, the likelihood of all the lead bits in some position being a one is the bias raised to the length of the input stream. For the parameters previously mentioned, $0.9^{1024} \approx 1.4 \, 10^{-47}$; the odds of that happening in any of our 128 sample positions is still less than $1.8 \, 10^{-45}$, so it is quite unlikely that we would ever encounter this for a realistic-sized corpus of inputs. If we shorten the length of inputs it becomes considerably more likely; if we increase the bias too much, it also becomes a lot more likely.

To see that, consider a bias of 127 out of 128. The probability that some given sample results in 1,024 values all of which begin with a one is now roughly $3.25 \, 10^{-4}$; the probability that at least one of our 128 samples has this property is now slightly more than 1 in 25, which means that it certainly will happen, and often, for realistically sized corpora. Nonetheless, the cost of recovering from such situations may be sufficiently low that this approach is still a good idea: in particular, the cost of generating bits to break the tie is still only 2 bits in expectation, raising our cost only by about $\frac{1}{12}^{\text{th}}$ of a bit, for typical-sized documents; this is a small penalty on top of the 1.2 bits we already expect to pay.

But this is a good idea only if we can also resolve the first caveat: how do we efficiently produce the biased bits?

Rather than answer this directly, we return to our *gedankenexperiment*, and consider some consequences. If we could produce these biased bits, what is the likelihood of multiple values all starting with a one? For a bias of b, and a multiplicity value of m, this is just b^m. For example, suppose we pick $b = 1 - 1/m$; for our previous choice of bias, this would suggest choosing $m = 10$. But

$$\lim_{m \to \infty} \left(1 - \frac{1}{m}\right)^m = \frac{1}{e}$$

so all m values start with a one more than a third of the time. This convergence is reasonably rapid: for $m = 11$ and larger, the value of $\left(1 - \frac{1}{m}\right)^m$ exceeds 0.35; the limiting value of $\frac{1}{e}$ is about 0.367879. The value exceeds 0.36 starting at $m = 24$, and 0.365 starting at $m = 65$.

Given a value of m, we can break our set of samples into blocks of length m. Compute the binary expansion of $\left(1 - \frac{1}{m}\right)^m$. Generate uniformly distributed random bits while they equal the expansion; when they first differ, a 0 when we are trying to match a 1 indicates that the random number is smaller, and conversely. We expect to examine only two random bits to find the first point of divergence to effect a single comparison; again, if our random stream of bits is zero at the first bit that differs, then our random number is below the threshold and is otherwise larger.

Finding a value above the threshold means that at least one of our sequences starts with a biased zero. Using roughly $\log_2 m$ bits, identify that winner among the m sequences, generate bits until the next one bit to compute the number of leading zeros, and determine if there are more winners. Identifying the winner uses exactly $\log m$ bits when m is a power of 2, and at most twice that many bits in expectation by repeating a random draw until a previously unselected value is chosen (and reducing the range when half the numbers have been chosen). The probability of needing a second choice is the same, but with $m - 1$ replacing m in the exponent, resulting in a value exceeding $1/e$, causing the expected number of repetitions to be at most e.

Consequently, the number of bits needed to resolve all m samples for a given input is roughly $2 + e(\log_2 m + 2 + 2)$, plus whatever bits are needed to patch up the positions in which all values start with a one. For $m = 128$, this results in $2 + 11e = 31.9011$; the discrepancy between our target and $1/e$ and patching up the second and subsequent selections pushes this up slightly, but it remains smaller than 32. Thus, with an expected 32 bits of randomness we can usually resolve 128 samples for sufficiently long inputs; reducing to 2 batches with $m = 64$, brings us well under 64 bits, leading to an expectation of either $\frac{1}{4}$ or $\frac{1}{2}$ bit per input per sample, plus the corrections. The likelihood of needing correction at $m = 64$ is small: it will happen about once in a few thousand times; as previously noted, the probability of correction at $m = 128$ is significant, but amounts to under $\frac{1}{12}$ bit, increasing the total expected cost to $\frac{1}{3}$ or $\frac{7}{12}$ bit per input per sample, both of which are considerably less than 2. To make the math more rigorous, we can change the bias to $\frac{1}{\sqrt[m]{e}}$, and we can view the values as determining the smallest sample to start with a zero, by choosing the smallest k such that a random stream viewed as a binary fraction exceeds $1 - e^{-\frac{k}{m}}$ as the first value to start with a zero. We expect to repeat this choice until the smallest such k exceeds m, and we will need to examine slightly more than $\log_2 m$ bits to place the stream into the proper bin, all of which tightens up the math slightly, but leads to roughly the same answer.

To make this even more systematic, we note that, with a fixed bias b, the probability of exactly k leading zeros is $\binom{m}{k}(1 - b)^k b^{m-k}$ for any phrase. These terms sum to 1, being the summands of the binomial expansion of $((1 - b) + b)^k$. If we break the sum into pieces based on m, we see, if $b \approx \frac{1}{m}$, that the number of values selected to start with a zero is highly likely to be small; with the standard parameters of $m = 128, b = \frac{127}{128}$, we find that for each phrase, the probability of zero samples starting with a zero is 0.366437716. The probability of one sample starting with a zero is 0.369323052 (the most likely outcome); the probability of two and three are 0.184661526 and 0.061069166. The cumulative probability of any larger result is under $\frac{1}{2}$ of a percent. Within each range, we can continue to generate bits to sort the random value into $\binom{m}{k}$ equal-sized sub-bins to pick the winners. We then pay an additional cost of two expected bits to compute the values beyond the leading zeros in m positions, and $\log_2 \binom{m}{k}$ bits to find the correct slot. Since $\binom{m}{k}$ is less than m^k, this adds at most $\log_2 m^k = k \log_2 m = 7k$ extra bits; $9k$ after we take into account the extra bits needed to check for slot membership, using these . Multiplying these values by their probability in a spreadsheet, results in a limiting expected value of just under 18 bits to decide all 128 positions using the find k, and then sort out the $\binom{m}{k}$ winners and extended values approach.

We must still add the expected two bits per slot in the infrequent, but not rare, case that some slot has no winner, multiplying by the probability of such an event.

Sadly, few quality pseudo-random number generators exist which efficiently produce 32 bits with a large enough seed space to avoid collisions. Our experiments along these lines have looked at reduced versions of RC4, which have so far been successful at producing adequately random values, but which lose any cryptographic potency, and initializing the key space is still more work than one might like.

Recent papers by Pătraşcu and Thorup and others offer the hope that simple tabulation-based pseudo-random generators might be sufficient for our task, but at present this remains but a hope. The idea of these generators is to pick a small set of random tables (one for each byte position in the input), and compute the exclusive-or of the values in these tables.

4.3   FINDING THE FIRST POINT OF DIVERGENCE EFFICIENTLY

When comparing a random stream to a given binary number, we can compute the exclusive-or between the two, where the resulting random stream represents only the points of disagreement. In that case, it is interesting to count the number of zeros at the beginning of a random stream, so that we can focus on the position of the first one bit. This is the same operation needed when finding the initial sequence of zeros, using the expected two-bit generation scheme. In any case, it would be convenient, given a random stream, to quickly find the index of the earliest one bit.

This problem is reasonably well studied, although not as well remembered as it deserves. If we view the stream as the low-order bits of a base two number, simple arithmetic can help: `x & ((~x)+1)` isolates the lowest-order one in a binary word, if any (as in C, `&` is the bitwise `AND` operator, and `~` is the binary complementation operator). In C on a two's-complement machine (but not in Java), if `x` is an unsigned value, we could write `x & (-x)` to evaluate this; more-principled languages view the negation of an unsigned value as a bounds error.

Having done this for a word-sized chunk of our random stream, we can reduce the value to a power of 2 representing the right-most one in our word, or zero when there are no ones. The index problem is then equivalent to computing the integer base two logarithm of a power of two, shifting by that amount, and reporting the value, or refilling the word when it reaches zero, remembering the number of zeros seen so far reporting the sum of the stored zeros and the index of the rightmost one. There are a few tricks we might use to do this efficiently: if our word size is 64 bits, we might observe (as I was reminded by Peter Montgomery) that 2 is a primitive root of unity modulo 67, guaranteeing that modulo 67, the first 66 values of powers of 2 are all distinct and non-zero. To use this, take the power of 2 representing the least one, and compute the remainder modulo 67. Now look in a table of length 67 to determine the index.

Alternatively, we could use a De Bruijn sequence. A De Bruijn sequence is a string of letters from a given alphabet containing all k-letter strings from the alphabet exactly once, counting wrap-around (we imagine that the end of the sequence is followed by another copy of the sequence, as if attached to a necklace). In our case, we consider a binary alphabet, and strings of length six. The string of six zeros must occur someplace in a proper De Bruijn sequence of length 64 in this alphabet; we rotate the sequence so that it comes in the high-order bits, so that our De Bruijn sequence can be viewed as a 58 binary integer with a leading and trailing one, and no six consecutive zeros anywhere inside; denote this sequence by db. If we consider any small power of two times db and look at only the high-order six bits in the 64-bit product, we get a result which consists of consecutive bits of db. Because our De Bruijn sequence contains all strings of length six, we can construct a table mapping all six bit strings uniquely to the index which produces them as a result of this multiplication; this gives us a smaller table than the modular computation, and requires a multiplication instead of division, which is usually more efficient.

We might also note that $\log_2 64 = 6$. As a consequence, we can write a six-fold expression to compute the six bits of the logarithm of $x = 2^i$ by determining whether our given power of two is contained in the set of values which include that bit. For example, the lowest-order bit in the logarithm should be on for two, eight, thirty-two, etc. Computing `x & 0xAAAAAAAAAAAAAAAA` results in zero for even values of i, and non-zero otherwise. Other bits of i are similarly computed by using the masks `0xCCCCCCCCCCCCCCCC`, `0xF0F0F0F0F0F0F0F0`, `0xFF00FF00FF00FF00`, `0xFFFF0000FFFF0000`, and `0xFFFFFFFF00000000`. This has the unfortunate property of leading most naturally to a branching implementation, unless the compiler is clever enough to take advantage of native instructions for conditional moves or compare and swap, when these do not break pipelining.

In practice, however, since the strings we consider come from a uniform binary generator, we can avoid multiplication and division altogether by looking at the low-order byte of the value. When it is non-zero, use a table lookup to find the index of the rightmost one. When it is zero, which should happen only one time in 256, increase the zero counter by 8, and move to the next byte. This involves a slightly larger table lookup, but usually only one, and no multiplication or division. (The De Bruijn-variant was first noted by Randall et al., while considering efficient code for finding the activated bits in the return value from the UNIX `select` system call, in which the position of the first one depends on the file descriptor numbers attached to channels; if one of the channels happens to have a large number and a lot of activity, the byte-at-a-time method might prove to be more costly than the De Bruijn sequence.) One could imagine using a larger table to avoid the sporadic branches, but this may place too much pressure on the memory cache.

Note further that the byte-at-a-time approach will probably suffer a branch misprediction when the low-order byte is zero.

4.4   UNIFORM CONSISTENT SAMPLING SUMMARIZED

Assume a random stream generator which can be rapidly and efficiently reseeded. Posit a family of input streams of features each of length roughly 1,000. We want to consistently select from each input stream a set of 128 features uniformly with replacement, so that the Jaccard coefficient comparing the intersection and union of the contents of any pair of streams can be estimated without bias by the Jaccard coefficient of the vectors of samples.

Computing a random one-to-one function of each feature and picking the numerically smallest results in a consistent unbiased estimate of Jaccard. By lazily evaluating the function (looking for the longest leading string of zeros), we can reduce the expected number of bits evaluated to two, plus a few computations to break the unlikely ties. By lazily evaluating multiple functions at once, using a virtual biased leading bit, we can reduce the expected number of required random bits examined to approximately one-quarter for very long input streams, and one-third for streams of the posited typical input length.

CHAPTER 5

Why Weight (and How)?

The sampling mechanisms described in the previous sections provide unbiased estimators of the standard unweighted Jaccard coefficient, in which all features are treated as being equally important. But some features really are more important than other features: when seeking highly similar web pages, a matching document title may well provide a better indicator of similarity than a matching hyperlink. Phrases containing uncommon words may be better predictors of semantic proximity than common phrases.

One measure of the importance of a feature could be how many places it occurs in a document. In the sampling for the unweighted similarity we have already considered, the features are considered as a set, wherein repeated features collapse to a single representative. We could, however, view the features as a multi-set, that is, a bag in which elements can be repeated. To view our input as a set, we can imagine that the n_f^A occurrences of a feature f in a multiset A are separate features $f_1, f_2, \ldots, f_{n_f^A}$, where all the f_i are distinguishable, with f_n corresponding to selecting (f, n) as a sample. Computing the Jaccard coefficient using this expanded feature set is equivalent to computing a generalized Jaccard coefficient

$$\frac{\sum_{f \in A \cup B} \min(n_f^A, n_f^B)}{\sum_{f \in A \cup B} \max(n_f^A, n_f^B)}.$$

Note that for a standard set A, n_f^A, is equal to 1 when $f \in A$, and is equal to 0 otherwise. The min will equal 0 outside the intersection and 1 for features in the intersection; the max term will always be 1, since we have restricted our attention only to features present in at least one document. Consequently, the sum becomes a tally of the intersection divided by a tally of the union, reducing the formula to the conventional Jaccard coefficient computation. However, when applied to multi-sets, frequently occurring features gain increased importance.

This provides our first example of a weighted comparison, in which the weight of every feature is its frequency. In classical information retrieval, a variety of other weight assignments have been studied. Notable among these is *TF-IDF* (term frequency times inverse document frequency) in which the number of occurrences of a feature in a document is divided by the number of documents in the entire corpus which contain that feature at least once, or other variants such as dividing by the frequency in the entire corpus, or taking the logarithm of the fraction, or any number of other variations. Commonly, this is applied to documents viewed as bags of individual words, where we can see how this aids in the automatic deprecation of commonplace (or *stop*) words. For example, the word the, while it may occur dozens of times in a typical 1000-

word document, will also occur in almost every English-language document in a corpus, not to mention the smaller number of French-language documents (if accents are suppressed during normalization) discussing tea. Modern web corpora contain tens of billions of documents, making the TF-IDF value for a widely popular word like the very small. In contrast, the score for aardvark or wildebeest will be much larger, as very few documents refer to aardvarks[1] or wildebeests.[2] We will offer further superficial consideration of both below.

Let us first consider the discrete process described above (that is, one in which the weights are integers). For concreteness, let's take our features to be types of animals: cat, dog, aardvark, and wildebeest. We view the weights as being the number of each type of animal in our collection, and number the animals from zero to the weight of that animal (measured by frequency or importance, not physical weight); thus, W_{aardvark}, when the animal is an aardvark. Slightly altering our original design, and making the conventional term min-hashing even less appropriate, we would choose for each W_{aardvark} a uniform random number in the interval from 0 to 1, and choose the aardvark with the *largest* random number.

In order to achieve an exact approximation of Jaccard, the earlier argument still applies: if samples are uniform (relative to share of weight) and consistent (as weights are reduced, samples change only when the previous sample is no longer available), then equal samples occur in two weighted documents with probability equal to the Jaccard coefficient. To speed this up, we consider what the overall effect is: a sequence of random numbers is selected for our input set. At some points in the sequence, a new maximal value is selected, which remains maximal for a while.

5.1   CONSTANT EXPECTED-TIME CONSISTENT WEIGHTED SAMPLING

Following Gollapudi and Panigrahy, call an index at which a new maximal value occurs an *active index*. By uniformity, the active indices can be seen to be geometrically distributed: when the weight is 1, the only index available is 0, and whatever random value is chosen establishes a new maximum. With weight 2 or larger, when we consider index 1, by uniformity, the probability of 1 becoming the next active index after 0 must be one-half (since only zero and one are available). Similarly, index k becomes active with probability $\frac{1}{k}$. Consequently, when considering only the indices from $2^i + 1$ to 2^{i+1}, at least one of these is active with probability one-half.

This leads to a technique for improving the efficiency of selecting values: determine the set of active indices between $2^i + 1$ and 2^{i+1} by picking a random real value r between 0 and 1. When $r \leq 0.5$, there are no active indices in the specified range. Otherwise, decide that $a =$

---

[1]Since this document now scores highly for aardvark, I feel compelled to provide a smidgeon of useful information to those unfortunate enough to have inadvertently stumbled across it in the hope of learning some choice details about the animal. Sadly, my knowledge scarcely extends beyond that of a dictionary: to wit, an aardvark is a burrowing mammal found primarily in sub-Saharan Africa with sharp strong claws, a long nose, and a long tongue, all used primarily for finding, capturing, and consuming ants and termites. I have even less to report about echidnas, numbats, or other animals often described as anteaters (despite differing due to possessing teeth). Such variety in ant-consuming mammals is unsurprising, once you know that ants comprise roughly a fifth of the total terrestrial animate biomass. Thank you, Wikipedia.

[2]The Flanders and Swann song *I'm a Gnu* would be far less euphonious had it been entitled *I'm a Wildebeest*.

$\lceil 2^{i+1} r \rceil$ is the largest active index in $(2^i, 2^{i+1}]$. Pick a new r, and see if $r(a - 1) > 2^i$. If so, $\lceil r(a - 1) \rceil$ is the next-smaller active index, and repeat until the product falls below the lower threshold. In this way, we can find the active indices immediately below and above weight w with an expected constant amount of work: each power-of-two-sized interval contains an active index with probability one-half, and, in expectation, enumerating the active indices in an interval takes at most two iterations (as a decreases, the probability of exceeding 2^i decreases, so an iteration is terminal with probability at least one-half).

The value v associated with index 0 can be taken as a uniformly chosen random number in the unit interval. The value associated with the next larger active index is a random number between v and 1. Following this approach, Sreenivas Gollapudi and Rina Panigrahy came up with a logarithmic-time algorithm for producing active indices and associated hash values: find all active indices below a given weight, and select increasing random numbers for each of them. In expectation, for integer weights (or even for arbitrary real weights greater than any fixed positive value), there will be logarithmically many active indices.

We hoped to do better: we want an expected constant-time algorithm for finding the hash value associated with the active index immediately smaller than a given weight, for arbitrary non-negative weights. Because of the way the hash values are determined, this is just finding the second-largest hash value produced, given that the largest is produced at index z, the active index immediately larger than our given weight.

Using the uniform distribution to individually select z values, we first note that a single value is chosen to be smaller than x with probability x, so the probability that the value at every position other than i is x or smaller is x^{z-1}. Consequently, the probability that all z values are less than x is x^z. There are z choices for i, and the second-largest is smaller than x either when all of the values are smaller than x, or for some i, all others are smaller, but (with probability $1 - x$) value i is not. Consequently, the probability that the second-largest value fails to exceed x is $z(1 - x)x^{z-1} + x^z = zx^{z-1} - (z - 1)x^z$.

Given this formula for a cumulative distribution, we can choose a second-largest value by picking a probability p uniformly, and finding the value of x which results in a cumulative probability of p, using binary search to find x quickly when we need to know the value (by the nature of a cumulative distribution function or CDF, the function increases monotonically from 0 to 1 with x).

As we look to the continuous version of this, we can replace the single choice for index i with choices for some suitably large multiplier k of values for indices, $ki, ki + 1, \ldots, ki + k - 1$. To preserve the distribution of values in this interval, choose random values, and raise them to the k'th power. We do this because the cumulative distribution of the maximum of several independent values is the product of the cumulative distributions of the values: for the maximum to be less than some x, all of the values are less than that x. Doing this, and computing the distribution for second-largest values, there are now kz choices for i, and the resulting distribution function is $kz \left(1 - x^{\frac{1}{k}}\right) x^{z - \frac{1}{k}} + x^z = k \left(zx^{z - \frac{1}{k}} - (z - \frac{1}{k}) x^z\right)$. In this way, after changing active indices to include fractional values, we can deal efficiently with scaled fractional values.

If we remove the ceiling function, we can extend the set of active indices to allow arbitrary non-negative weights: weight zero indicates that a term should never be a sample; for larger weight, we need only find the intervals containing the active index below and above w, not all of the active indices. The computation remains the same, except that we remove the ceiling functions, the top of the range becomes ra instead of $r(a - 1)$, and we exclude 1 from the range of r.

By taking the limit as k approaches infinity, and ignoring all discretization in the generation of active indices, we find that the continuous cumulative distribution function is $F_z(x) = (1 - \ln x^z)x^z$. Again, to pick a value for item x, we choose a uniform value β_x and find $F_z^{-1}(\beta_x)$.

By monotonicity of the CDF in z, we note that we can often compare two such values without inversion: if $F_w\left(F_z^{-1}(\beta_x)\right) > \beta_y$, we can apply F_w^{-1} to both sides to learn if $F_w^{-1}(\beta_y) < F_z^{-1}(\beta_x)$ (monotonicity of the CDF allows us to get the comparison correct) and that therefore (x, z) is preferable to (y, w), without computing any inversions not already known to us; if the inequality goes the other way, we will probably need to invert (y, w) soon, since it is probably preferable to (x, z). If we process elements in order of decreasing weight, we can hope to further reduce the number of times an inversion is needed to determine an ordering, since increasing weight increases the expected value.

Since we have almost exactly mirrored the selection of many values, we have consistency and weighted uniformity for free, but let us prove them anyway: consistency follows from the generation of active indices and from monotonicity of $F_w(\beta)$ in both w and β. The active index selected for any feature is the one immediately below the weight of that feature, using the active index immediately above as key for generation of the value. If the weight distribution changes for some feature, the selected value remains the same as long as the weight remains above the preceding active index, and decreasing weights (due to monotonicity) only decreases the weight of candidate values.

By construction of the active indices, given an active index z, the active index immediately preceding z is a uniform distribution of numbers between 0 and z. Thus, to prove weighted uniformity, it is sufficient to prove that, given a weight distribution $S(x)$, the probability of selecting (x, w) for some w is equal to the proportion of the weight attributable to x, i.e., $\frac{S(x)}{\sum S(y)}$.

To prove this, we would like to measure the probability, averaged over all choices of z and β_x that the hash value selected is maximal. To do this, we consider the cumulative density function $C_{S(x)}(v)$ for the value selected assuming weight $S(x)$ and chosen values less than v, which is $\int_{S(x)}^{\infty} p_{S(x)}(z) F_z(v) dv$, where $p_{S(x)}(z)$ is the probability density that the active index immediately following $S(x)$ occurs at z. Looking at the discrete case, we see that $p_{S(x)}(z) = \frac{S(x)}{z(z-1)}$; this follows because the probability of z being active, if it is larger than $S(x)$, is $\frac{1}{z}$, and, to be the next active index, no index between $S(x)$ and z can be active, which happens with probability $\prod_{S(x) < z' < z} \left(1 - \frac{1}{z'}\right)$ which telescopes to $\frac{S(x)}{z-1}$, resulting in a probability density of $\frac{S(x)}{z(z-1)}$. The fractional case (stepping by $\frac{1}{k}$) leads to a density of $\frac{S(x)}{z(z-\frac{1}{k})}$, which tends to $\frac{S(x)}{z^2}$ in the limit as k becomes large.

Substitution and the observation that $\frac{d(-\frac{v^z}{z})}{dz} = \frac{v^z}{z^2} - \frac{v^z \ln v}{z} = \frac{v^z(1 - \ln v^z)}{z^2}$ yield

$$C_{S(x)}(v) = S(x) \int_{S(x)}^{\infty} \frac{v^z(1 - \ln v^z)}{z^2} dz = S(x) \frac{-v^z}{z}\Big|_{S(x)}^{\infty} = S(x)\frac{v^z}{z}\Big|_{\infty}^{S(x)} = v^{S(x)}$$

for $0 \leq v \leq 1$. This is what should have been expected: it should be the same as computing the distribution of the minimum of $S(x)$ uniformly distributed values, ignoring the existence of active indices.

By taking the derivative, we note that the probability density function of producing exactly value v is $S(x)v^{S(x)-1}$. Summing over the possible values for the minimum over all input features, we find that the probability that feature x produces the minimum value v is the density above times the probability of all others being larger

$$\int_0^1 S(x)v^{S(x)-1} \prod_{y \neq x} v^{S(y)} dv = S(x) \int_0^1 v^{-1+\sum S(y)} dv = \frac{S(x)}{\sum S(y)} v^{\sum S(y)}\Big|_0^1 = \frac{S(x)}{\sum S(y)}$$

as desired to establish weighted uniformity.

For consistency to hold, we must still select pseudo-randomness leading to the same choices when presented with sub-distributions of weight. In particular, consistency will occur if we rely only on x and some specified rounded values of $S(x)$ to decide which active indices in the vicinity of $S(x)$ are closest above (producing z) and closest below (determining the sample weight y). Since the computations of y and z are needed only once we have chosen the feature which produces the maximal value, we can defer computation of the sample weight until immediately prior to returning the sample. We do need to pick a sample weight; without a sample weight, no meaningful definition of consistency can be made.

5.2 CONSTANT TIME CONSISTENT WEIGHTED SAMPLING

Following Sergey Ioffe (who followed our above line of reasoning fairly closely in his paper), we can come at this in another way, using exponentially distributed values instead of uniformly distributed ones. In proving that we accurately estimate the Jaccard coefficient, we have seen that only uniformity and consistency are required, nothing about the actual values being bounded or nicely distributed. In an exponential distribution with rate s, values are distributed between 0 and ∞. The probability that a value smaller than x is chosen, is $\text{cdf}_s(x) = 1 - e^{-sx}$. This gives us a complementary CDF (CCDF) of e^{-sx} and a complementary CDF that k samples with exponential rate s all exceed x of e^{-skx}, an exponential CCDF with rate sk. When choosing a sample, we can use a complementary cumulative distribution in place of a cumulative distribution, so we can select value a by choosing a number u uniformly in the unit interval, and picking a so that $1 - cdf_s(a) = ccdf_s(a) = u$. For a rate s distribution, that leads to $u = e^{-sa}$, so $\ln u = -sa$, or $a = -\frac{\ln u}{s}$.

Using these exponential distributions, we can consider the more-conventional minimum of our random values, which we can now find using closed-form expressions, as follows.

Given a single item x, and a weight $w = S(x)$, the random value a_x (which for brevity, we will write as a when unambiguous) associated with x can be chosen by evaluating $a = -\frac{\ln u_x}{w}$. In this, u_x (which we henceforth write as u for simplicity) is a uniform unit interval value chosen for x independent of $S(x)$ and the choices of y and z. This formula results from inverting the CCDF as above, using the item weight as a rate.

We know that a remains smallest up to weight z. This tells us that all values in an interval of weights ranging from w up to z exceed a. Using the CCDF again, and noting that the CCDF is monotonic in z, we find that $a = -\frac{\ln u'_x}{z-w}$, where u'_x (henceforth written u') is a second random value chosen from the unit interval, showing that a is achieved at z, and no smaller value occurs between w and z.

Cross-multiplying and adding, we get $wa + (z - w)a = za = -\ln u - \ln u'$, hence $a = -\frac{\ln u + \ln u'}{z}$. We note that the values chosen for different values of x are independent; the values chosen for x and different weights depend only on z, forming a decreasing step function of minima as z increases. Choosing a in this way, we need only find the active indices, and choose two uniform random values for each feature to choose the smallest hash value.

Further following Ioffe, we can reconsider our mechanism for selecting y and z. We know that y is a uniformly distributed value in the range $[0, w)$, so $y = vw$, for a newly selected uniform unit interval random value v. But w is also uniformly distributed below z: consider the CCDF, where the probability that the smallest value between 0 and z occurs before w is $\frac{w}{z}$. Now, this is the CCDF for the location of the next larger active index, z. As such, a uniform unit value can be used to locate z, yielding $z = \frac{w}{v'}$. To achieve consistency, the selection of y and z need to be the same for large runs of w; fortunately, by dividing the two equations, we learn that $\frac{y}{z} = vv' = r$, which is now independent of w.

Having selected $q = \frac{1}{r} = \frac{z}{y}$, note that $y \le w \le z = qy$, so $1 \le \frac{w}{y} \le q$. Consequently, $0 \le \log_q \frac{w}{y} \le 1$. Considering the density functions, we find that $\log_q \frac{w}{y}$ should be uniform in $(0, 1)$, to get uniform probability for all y in $[rw, w)$. But we still need consistency, so that the same value of y is chosen for all w between y and qy. To achieve this, let β be a uniform unit value in $[0, 1)$. Note that $\lceil \log_q w + \beta \rceil - \beta$ is uniformly distributed in $[\log_q w - 1, \log_q w)$. Taking $\log_q y = \lceil \log_q w + \beta \rceil - \beta$ we find $y = q^{\lceil \log_q w + \beta \rceil - \beta}$, and $z = yq = q^{1 + \lceil \log_q w + \beta \rceil - \beta}$. Note that this achieves uniformity: setting w' to any value between y and z (excluding z) produces something with base q logarithm in the range

$$[\lceil \log_q w + \beta \rceil - \beta, 1 + \lceil \log_q w + \beta \rceil - \beta) .$$

Any logarithm of a weight w' in this range results in the same values being produced for y and z, yielding the desired uniformity properties and consistency.

Consequently, we can find a, y, and z by choosing five random unit variables, u, u', v, v', and β. We then compute $q = vv'$ (and $r = \frac{1}{vv'}$), and set $c = -\ln u - \ln u'$.

In code, we can produce a list rand of pseudo-random unit numbers seeded by the feature, select five numbers at a time, and compute:

```
double u1 = rand[offset++];
double u2 = rand[offset++];
double v1 = rand[offset++];
double v2 = rand[offset++];
double beta = rand[offset++];

double q = v1*v2;
double c = -Math.Log(u1) - Math.Log(u2);

double t = Math.Floor(beta - Math.Log(weight, q));
double y = Math.Pow(q, beta - t);
double z = y / q;
return c / z; // a
```

5.3   ACCELERATING WEIGHTED SAMPLING

We don't know of any techniques to make weighted sampling fully as efficient as the unweighted case, but we can improve the use of randomness considerably.

When selecting multiple samples, we can compute several values of β_x in parallel using the expected two-bit technique described in discussing the weighted case: generate a pseudo-random bit sequence keyed on x and split the sequence into sequences of ones terminated by the first zero (since we now look for maximal values, β values near one are the most desirable). We can terminate production of β values at this point, having bounded the region in which β_x lies; with this restriction, and a precise value of z, we can use the substitution method with the low and high bounds on β_x to see if the values straddle the previous best. When they do, we need to generate more bits, but we can place the candidates in a queue, and hope that a subsequent x will produce a clearly larger value.

We can also estimate z closely in parallel: generate m pseudo-random bits based on x and on $\lceil \log_2 S(x) \rceil + k$ for the needed values of k: in expectation $O(\log m)$ of them when picking m samples. Use these bits to determine if an active index falls into the corresponding binary interval. To preserve consistency, we use all m bits, even when only a few of them are still needed to find a non-empty interval. To reduce the frequency of reseeding the generator, generate batches of $km \log m$ bits, for powers of two intervals $2^{ki}, 2^{ki} + 1, \ldots, 2^{ki+k-1}$. When $k \approx \log m$, we can hope to need only a small constant number of batches; for typical values of m (say around 128), the batches can be taken to be roughly a 1,000 bits long, and 2 or 3 batches will usually suffice, giving an expected number of reseedings to compute a coarse approximation to both β_x and z of 3, and an expected number of bits needed per sample of roughly 15. Experimentally, especially if the features are first sorted with largest weights first, using these coarse estimates of β_x and z, we find that the number of pairs we need to compute precisely is rarely more than double the number of pairs we would have needed had β_x and z been specified to infinite precision, even without buffering (where we increase precision of both the current leader and the candidate to the point where we can decide which should be the new leader); since the expectation of z is unbounded, keeping a buffer and waiting for a sufficiently large z is likely to reduce the computation needed. Note that, unless $S(x)$ is a power of two, we can't be sure if an active index in the first interval establishes an upper bound on z without determining whether the largest active index in the enclosing interval is greater than $S(x)$. Nonetheless, we can often eliminate candidate samples with little effort.

Turning to the constant-time variant, we know desirable properties in particular, if given q and β) is independent of w, for $w \in [y, z]$ that is, we find (if we set an initial y_0, corresponding to the active index preceding 1) that we can choose y and z from the geometric series $\ldots, r^2 y_0, r y_0, y_0, \frac{y_0}{r}, \frac{y_0}{r^2}, \ldots$ so that they bracket w, by computing $\lfloor \log_r w \rfloor$. Since y_0 is the largest active index smaller than 1, and since y_0 should be uniform in $[0, 1)$, it should also be uniform in $[r, 1)$. Since w is a likely given to us a floating point number, we can usually compute the base-2 logarithm of w just from the exponent field, which should allow us to get close to y and z quite effectively. Nonetheless, we find that, in practice, choosing y_0, u, u', v, and v' uniformly requires a lot of effort. The remaining computations of logarithms, sums, and divisions are relatively inexpensive, so a closed-form method of selecting samples remains appealing, if given a free source of pseudo-randomness.

CHAPTER 6

A Few Applications

In this chapter, we look, or in some cases look yet again, at a few of the applications we have made of these and other sampling techniques.

In the first section, we once again consider web page deduplication for a search engine; this time, we delve a little deeper into some of the practical issues involved.

In the second section (Section 6.2), we turn to a different domain in which sampling has been of use: deduplication and single-instance storage of file systems. In this case, our concern is not with annoying the user by presenting multiple nearly identical copies, but with conserving disk space and network bandwidth when dealing with file systems containing copies and differing versions of files.

6.1   WEB DEDUPLICATION

Harkening back, the first application of efficient near-duplicate detection we examined was a problem we encountered when first launching the Alta Vista search engine. Although the initial corpus was small by modern standards (about thirty million pages), it still contained a large number of duplicate and near-duplicate web pages. Identical pages are fairly easy to recognize: a simple fingerprint of the contents of every page can tell us when two pages are highly likely to be identical. Adding this fingerprint was relatively inexpensive (every page needs to be crawled and indexed anyway, so computing a simple fingerprint can be done at little extra cost; storing a fingerprint uses less space than storing the URL of a page).

Full-page fingerprinting eliminated many user complaints, but not all: we quickly found out that exact-duplicate detection had eliminated an average of two copies of those pages with duplicates. That is, we found that about one-fifth of the pages in our corpus were exact duplicates; the number depended strongly on the query, and, since the service was still in limited-release, we did not have reliable dynamic frequency information on queries at that time, just the comments from some of our beta users.

Nonetheless, we were still receiving user complaints about result pages containing repetitive answers. Quick inspection convinced us that the pages in question did differ, but often in limited or inconsequential ways. Users were nearly as annoyed by reading links pointing to highly related pages as they were by links to identical pages. We decided to look for measurements that characterized user dissatisfaction, and found that, for the most part, user unhappiness was well-correlated to high Jaccard similarity between pages. This correlation is imperfect: two pages which differ only in the inclusion of the word **not** in one may well be viewed as dissimilar, despite having a high Jaccard coefficient. We found whole categories of pages in which Jaccard agreement was a very bad proxy for near-duplication: our favorite examples of pages where Jaccard was a poor measure were catalog pages in which the navigational content dominates the informational content, by word count. Nonetheless, a user might expect to retrieve listings for more than one brand-name coffee shop in a large city; since 95% or more of the words on every page describing each shop were the taxonomy and navigational structure, a simple Jaccard computation was already known to be imperfect.

Still, the static evidence was clear: we could find another sixth of our corpus to be duplicates by computing Jaccard coefficients, and eliminating those pages with similarity in the range of 95% or more. All that remained was to find an efficient way of comparing millions of web pages to one another, finding almost all pairs of pages with high Jaccard similarity, and very few with similarity scores below roughly 70%.

To do this, we turned to supershingling—a way of summarizing samples efficiently. Suppose that two documents have similarity p. By construction of our samples, this means that in each sample position we have matching samples with probability p. The probability of k independent samples matching is then p^k; for no particularly good reason, other than simple calculation, if $p = 0.95$, $p^{14} \approx 0.5$. As a consequence, if we divide our samples into blocks of length 14, and compute a hash function of the samples in each block, we expect those hash values to coincide roughly half the time for pairs of documents with Jaccard similarity of 95%, and more often for pages with higher similarity, but far less often for pages with lower similarity; for example, $0.7^{14} \approx 0.007$, and $0.5^{14} \approx 0.00006$, so even if pages with middling Jaccard similarity were common, we would rarely misidentify them as duplicates.

As a consequence, if we compute 6 hash values of 14 non-overlapping consecutive samples, and ask for at least 2 of the 6 to agree, the binomial theorem (and inclusion/exclusion) tells us this happens with probability $1 - (1 - p^{14})^6 - 6p^{14}(1 - p^{14})^5 = 1 - (1 - p^{14})^5(1 + 5p^{14})$. For, $p = 0.95, 0.7$, and 0.5, this results in detection probabilities of approximately 87%, 0.7%, and 0.006%, which seemed pretty good.

In reworking this for Microsoft Search (better known now as Bing), we wanted to remedy some of the problems with this: storing 6 hash values to 64 bits of precision takes 48 bytes of storage, which may not seem like much, but storing that much for every page starts to consume significant memory. Moreover, the Search team wanted to do a better job with near-duplicates; they wanted to eliminate only those results matching the query from consideration, rather than permanently shrinking the corpus. To do this efficiently, we wanted to be able to hold all of the super-shingle values in the distributed memory of the machines holding the referenced set of pages; since each machine was slated to hold about fifty million pages, this meant that each machine would need to dedicate over two gigabytes of memory just to holding supershingle values. Since each machine under consideration was meant to have only four gigabytes of memory, this was deemed to be undesirable. Something had to be done.

We resolved this by storing six 16-bit super-shingle values instead, cutting the memory burden to a quarter of the naïve requirement. Asking that at least two such values match seemed a bit too easy: it could happen purely by accident for one pair of pages in a few billion. Since the number of potential pairs was expected to be in the billions of billions, this seemed a little generous. Consequently, we reduced the length of expected matches from 14 to 5, but asked that 4 of the 6 values agree. This shifted the curves a little bit, but still within tolerance, and allowed us to dynamically retrieve the supershingles for pages at the time of index inspection when looking for matching pages. We could then compare the retrieved supershingles, looking for matches.

We used one further trick, both at Alta Vista, and for Microsoft Search: we took advantage of the fact that both six choose two and six choose four are 15, a relatively small number. When considering a set of pages, we compute all 15 interesting subsets of supershingles, and populate a hash table with the 64-bit concatenation of the 4 16-bit values (in the case of Microsoft Search), or a new hash value computed from the two 64-bit values (for Alta Vista). We then looked for any collisions in the hash tables as evidence of a sufficient degree of agreement.

6.2   FILE SYSTEMS: WINNOWING AND FRIENDS

In the above application, we have considered only finding samples distributed evenly by weight. In some application we may prefer to locate samples more smoothly; as noticed by Schleimer, Wilkerson, and Aiken, and subsequently by Teodosiu et al., placing samples uniformly with probability p means that no sample is chosen by position m with probability $(1 - p)^m$. Choosing $m \approx 1/p$, we find that with probability $(1 - \frac{1}{m})^m \approx \frac{1}{e}$ no choice is made within distance m; with probability approximately $\frac{1}{e^k}$, no choice is made by km. This exponential drops fairly slowly, so while the average distance between samples is m, we may commonly find samples as far apart as $10m$ in large files ($e^{10} \approx 20,000$; if a typical interval places samples from files at distance 1,000, a file of size 20 megabytes is very likely to contain some consecutive samples at distance 10,000 or more). For Schleimer et al., looking for evidence of plagiarism in student programming assignments, this meant that it would have been too easy to overlook strong evidence of cheating. They thus defined a new algorithm, *winnowing*, for selecting interesting locations in files, with controlled maximal distance between samples, but with consistent selection of samples to increase the likelihood of finding pairs.

In winnowing, we compute a hash function on a short sliding window of text, looking not for specific values modulo m, but rather for the rightmost smallest value in a window of length m. If the input data is random, by choosing the short windows and the hash function of appropriate lengths, we can make it highly unlikely that any collisions will occur; on less-random input, we can set parameters making it likely that collisions occur (with high probability) only when the input text repeats itself. By choosing the rightmost such value in the window, we ensure that on highly repetitive text that the interval between samples will be approximately m; on random input, the interval will be approximately $\frac{m}{2}$ on average, ignoring the effect that the items in the portion of the outer window following the selection point are known to have larger values. After the selection of a sample, we can look at all the next m positions to find the location for the next sample.

The location of the rightmost minimum within the outer window is a *cut-point*; the location of the smallest to the right of a cut-point is a candidate for the location of the next cut-point. By maintaining a ring buffer of size m of locations and hash values, with the minimal hash value at the start of the ring, and positions increasing in both location and hash value following the minimal, we can maintain this list with at most three amortized comparison operations per location: read the next byte, compute the hash value corresponding to the run of bytes terminating with the new byte using a sliding window hash function, as described above in Section 2.2. If the hash value is minimal (including a tie for minimal, or if the ring buffer is empty, as happens initially or when the preceding minimum was located at the end of the window), reset the ring buffer with the new value in the first position. Otherwise, examine the ring buffer one position at a time from the large end, looking for a smaller value.

When found (as it will be, since the new value is not smallest), insert the new value and position in the next spot in the ring buffer, discarding all elements of the ring currently at that point or later. Each position is thus compared at most twice when inserted (once to see if it is minimal and once as larger than an element in the ring), and at most once when deleted, when losing to a subsequent value. We could use a binary search to find the proper location, which would improve the worst case time at the cost of the average (the list can be expected to be of length $O(\log_2 m)$); if we only count hash comparisons, and are willing to be careful about falling off the front of ring buffer, we could reduce the amortized cost to two, by allowing elements to bubble to the front of the ring; the current approach seems easier to code correctly, dealing with the case of a new minimum along with the case of an empty ring, so I prefer this. If our comparison function allows for a sentinel value, guaranteed to compare as smaller than any true value, we could place such a sentinel at the front of the ring (and inserting an extra sentinel whenever the ring rotates due to deletion of the element following the sentinel), this would remain easy to compute.

If the hash values happen to occur in increasing order (very unlikely in non-adversarial situations), the ring may grow as long as m elements, but for random values, we expect to reach only $O(\log m)$, so the cache behavior of this should be quite good, usually referencing only the start of the ring, and a few positions near the tail. In repeated experiments with pseudo-random data, looking at nearly a trillion sequences of length 2^m, we never found the need for a buffer larger than $4 + 3\log_2 m$, but the probability is non-zero, so it is undoubtedly best to err on the side of safety).

Picking interesting locations in this way, we find that the set of marked locations moves along with the input: if a few bytes are inserted at the front of a file, the cut-points will (unless the new bytes are lucky enough to land in the middle of a cut-point) move to the new positions of the matching data. If a few bytes are changed, they are unlikely to introduce new local minima, or to have been selected from the small window defining a cut-point. Even if they are, other nearby cut-points will have moved with their data, so we expect that small edits will mostly preserve the contents of inter-cut-point segments of files; the probability of this (for a single edit) is proportional to the length of a local hash location divided by the typical length of a segment.

Taking advantage of this, Teodosiu et al. defined *differential compression* on files using these winnowing-derived cut-points, and cryptographically strong checksums of the inter-cut-point segment, which they called *chunks*. They further defined *recursive differential compression*, by considering the sequence of chunk signatures as a new input stream, to be further subdivided using recursive application of the winnowing technique (but now to sequences of chunk signatures). They then considered file transmission between machines by transferring the root of the tree of checksums: a checksum of the whole file. If that was a match for any file currently known to the recipient, stop: declare the new file to be equal to the matching file. If not, send the hash values of the chunks at the top-level of recursion. For any previously known checksums, retrieve the original data; for any unknown ones, request the contents recursively, as either a list of checksums, or actual data. This is related to the well-known idea of Merkle trees. In any case, this greatly reduces the communication required when sending a new file which is a small edit of an old file. It does require a few round trips to communicate the path of mismatched checksums, but the latency of this can be hidden within the transmission of other files, if synchronizing an entire file system, rather than a single file. If not, Michael Mitzenmacher has written a number of co-authored papers on Counting Bloom Filters, which have been adapted to help solve this problem, given an upper-bound on the number of unmatched chunks, using group-coding techniques to allow for the simultaneous transmission of a small set of values given shared knowledge of a large set.

This is where things were when I stepped in (at Dan Teodosiu's invitation). Dan asked me if, rather than indexing all of the chunk checksums in a file system, we could use chunk signatures to hint at other files likely contain matching chunks: given memory constraints, the alternative (as originally implemented) was to consider only the chunks in the existing copy of a given file.

This led to another application of similarity detection: consider a file to be represented by its sequence of chunk checksums, and the length of each chunk. Using this as the input stream to a Jaccard estimator, we can build short consistent sets of samples, where the samples are chosen to match with probability approximating the Jaccard similarity of the underlying stream of chunks. To fit within the available memory bounds, we chose 12 samples for each file, and for each of the samples 6 new bits were chosen, using a pseudo-random generator seeded with the fingerprint of the chunk. Sixty-three times out of 64, a match of the 6 bits in any single position then suggested a match of the chunks, suggesting a match of the chunk streams. One time in 64, a match would occur purely by chance in files without matching chunks. If the Jaccard similarity of two chunk streams was p, then the probability of agreement in the six-bit values would be $p + \frac{1-p}{64} = \frac{63p+1}{64}$, differing from p by $\frac{1-p}{64}$, which is rare enough that not too many false positives slip through; in more recent work described above, I mention König and Li's careful analysis of reduced-bit similarity-testing.

We then built 12 inverted indices, mapping the twelve 6-bit values to identifiers for the files in which they were selected, and used set-intersection techniques (namely, merge sort) to construct lists of those files with 1, 2, 3, and up to 12 features in common. We then chose our candidate files from the lists with the greatest numbers of common features, until we had found the desired number of candidate files.

Since the number of files in a file system (unlike the number of chunks) is only in the millions, none of these lists could exceed that number in length. Considering only accidental collisions, the expected number of common values is the number of files divided by 64. Any true matches beyond that are helpful in compressing transmission. Given the anticipated number of files, we are likely to find four accidental collisions in some files with no common chunks, but are unlikely to find more; correspondingly, we are very likely to find most files with more than one-third common chunks in one of the lists corresponding to five or more common chunk hashes.

Once these files are identified, we fetch the chunk signature lists for these files, and look for matching chunks in the newly transmitted files, using the matching chunks to avoid sending known values.

More recently, I was working with the Windows group on even faster techniques to perform the underlying chunking; this chunking can be costly, because we compute high-precision hash values in order to select winning locations. The group (Ahmed El-Shimi, Ran Kalach, Ankit Kumar, Jin Li, Adi Oltean, and Sudipta Sengupta) proposed a clever change, analogous to one we had used in Alta Vista: imagine that the hash function is composed of a short high-order portion, and a long low-order portion. Compute the high-order eight bits in every case, and fully evaluate only those inputs where it evaluates to zero: for those, compute the low-order part, and perform winnowing as usual. For the remainder, remember them until a location evaluating to zero in the high-order part is found, and compute low-order extensions only when the window is exhausted without having located any high-order winners.

I pointed out that this is suspect due to both the laws of probability and the nature of actual data files. To the latter, first: real-life files are often lower-entropy than random files would be—executable binaries often, for example, contain modest-length blocks of zeros to initialize static arrays. Spreadsheet files are often quite sparse, containing many empty cells, and so, if stored uncompressed, will not contain a lot of apparent randomness. One consequence of this lack of randomness is that very few values may be produced by local hashing. This may well mean that there are significantly fewer than 256 hash values of local segments in large portions of a file, in which case the likelihood of any of them evaluating to zero is decreased.

Even when there is a local leading zero, once consumed, there may be no subsequent ones. Consequently, we need to either maintain a list of the smallest leading values observed, or recompute those lead bytes if we find ourselves without any viable candidates. Or we can redefine the mapping to say that the value is a leading byte of zeros when that occurs, and a leading byte of one in all other cases, which will force more evaluation in the rare cases when no leading zeros occur.

How rare is this? In real, low-entropy files, this may happen a lot, and no analytic process can help us. In high-entropy files, the probability of the high-order byte evaluating to zero is

$\frac{1}{256}$. The probability that the high-order byte is non-zero is thus $\frac{255}{256} = 1 - \frac{1}{256}$. The limit of $(1 - \frac{1}{n})^n = \frac{1}{e} \approx 0.3679$; at $n = 256$, we discover a value of 0.36716, low by a fraction of a percent. For this to happen in an extended window of $256k$ bytes, we raise this to the k. Hence, with a 1 kilobyte outer window, we can expect to find no lead bytes evaluating to zero approximately 1 time in 55 even with perfectly random input. For a 100 kilobyte window into a random file, we expect this virtually never: a few times in 10 raised to the 175th power; even at 10 kilobytes, this happens in approximately 4 windows out of 10 to the 18th power.

Using this approach, we can accelerate our winnowing by a factor of at least 256: use a short fast hash function to extract a lead byte. If the lead byte is non-zero, tentatively ignore that position, by tossing the location into a buffer indexed by the value. If the lead byte is zero, mark all the buffers as empty, and evaluate an extended hash function. Maintain a ring buffer of locations in increasing order and increasing secondary hash value.

Upon reaching the end of the outer window, pick the first element of the ring buffer, if there is one, and shift the ring, and restart. If the ring buffer is empty, find the non-empty buffer with lowest index, and evaluate the elements of it as candidates for the cut-points.

Prior to using winnowing to place cut-points fairly uniformly within files, we considered using weighted sampling based on the length of chunks to find good samples, under the assumption that finding a long match would be better than finding a short one. With winnowing, this is less necessary; a few chunks are unusually short, but no chunks are exceptionally long.

6.3 FURTHER APPLICATIONS

In a series of papers (the bibliography reference for Chum et al. should get you on the right track), investigators have used unweighted sampling to help locate similar images in large databases. In some pending work, Alonso and others at Bing are investigating examination of social media, short messages, and tweets for deduplication and clustering.

CHAPTER 7

Forks in the Road: Flajolet and Slightly Biased Sampling

As mentioned in the Forward (sic, as described on page xv), shortly after the initial version of this publication was placed in the hands of my publisher, I received a disconcerting preprint from Ping Li: he and his students had come up with a way to produce a sketch for unweighted sampling without replacement in time linear in the length of the document. Their paper proposed producing a sketch which might sometimes be underfull: in particular, for short documents, there might be (or must be, for very short documents) sample slots with no generated selection, particularly since it proposed sampling without replacement. Subsequent papers by Ping Li and other colleagues found unbiased estimators which correct for this deficiency, as mentioned below.

I then began to consider whether Ping's technique could be extended to handle the weighted-sampling case. A few months of initial investigations showed that the answer could not be simple: producing an unbiased estimator of weighted sampling is hard for sampling without replacement, because the samples must be assigned some weight, and no assignment of weights can be found without knowledge of which pair of documents are to be considered. I was able to conclusively prove that no such unbiased sketching scheme could exist, by producing counterexamples to the existence of such algorithms.

I once again called upon my colleague Kunal Talwar and a new postdoctoral hire, Bernhard Haeupler, to see if we could at least find a reasonable approximation scheme to weighted sampling. After a few days work, we found one: a biased sampling scheme for estimating weighted Jaccard, with a bias at most equal to the multiplicative inverse of the weight of the sets being sketched. Taking advantage of the scale invariance of Jaccard, we found, as described below, a scaling approach with ε-bias to the estimator adding a small additive constant (the multiplicative inverse of ε) to the running time.

After we found such a technique, I began explaining it to Edith Cohen, and started by describing Ping's unweighted sampling technique. She immediately noticed the resemblance to the performance-enhancing tricks in a paper of Flajolet and Martin, so we'll begin by explaining that paper, and the reasons why — although my colleagues and I had read and admired that paper — we had overlooked the connection to min-hashing.

7.1 FLAJOLET-MARTIN

In 1984, Flajolet and Martin [6] published their paper on approximately counting the number of distinct items in a long stream. This was, in effective disguise, one of the first algorithms to introduce min-hashing.

The basic technique would be a straightforward application of min-hashing: to estimate the number of distinct items in a stream, pick a hash function with uniform output in the unit interval. Given k distinct inputs, the expected value of the minimum of k uniform random elements in the unit interval is $1/k$. Thus, we can estimate the number of distinct elements as the reciprocal of the smallest value attained when hashing the input stream. By using a randomly selected fixed hash function, identical elements will map to identical values, and thus not affect the minimum hash value.

To speed things up, and increase the accuracy of the estimate, they recommended using some of the high-order bits of the hash value to select a bin into which the minimization was to be performed; if we strip off, say, the first eight bits of the hash value to select a bin number between 0 and 255, we can use a single hash value to get 256 estimates of $n/256$, where n is the number of distinct input values.

But Flajolet and Martin had not stated it this way. They recorded not the minimum of uniform values, but rather assumed a uniform bit generator, and computed thereby the exponent field of an exponentially distributed value, by finding the maximal number of initial zero bits, after first uniformly selecting a bin. By computing only the exponent field and ignoring the mantissa, this paper produced slightly worse estimates (but faster) and successfully obscured the relationship to min-hashing. In subsequent papers, Flajolet and others found improvements dealing with empty bins, as well as other ways to reduce the noisiness of these estimates.

7.2 LI'S REDISCOVERY

Ping Li et al. [16], in 2012, wrote a paper proposing one permutation hashing, using a similar binning technique (but mantissa-generating permutations) in order to find a large number of samples for a min-hash sketch with a single random computation. The earliest version was again subject to empty bins, which led to inferior estimates; subsequent papers (written after we had already found a different way to address this problem, to be explained in the next few sections) addressed this deficiency by proposing that empty bins be filled with the sample from the immediately previous non-empty bin, and they prove the numerical stability of such an approximation.

7.3 APPROXIMATION BY RANDOMIZED ROUNDING

I returned to Kunal Talwar, and suggested that we should at least find an approximation scheme with bounded error. He almost immediately proposed a fruitful direction of inquiry: use Raghavan's randomized rounding [23] to replace the real values of a weighting by integers. We knew (from my earliest paper in this area [2]) how to convert integer weighting to repeated inputs, and so the initial proposal was to use this technique and randomized rounding to reduce the input set of weights to a small number of repeated (but differentiated by weight tag, and therefore different random bin selection and hash value) input values.

7.4   SCALING

The remaining problem was to deal with empty bins, and to produce a large enough set of samples to give a good estimate of the weighted Jaccard value. Shortly after the arrival of Bernhard Haeupler as a postdoctoral member of the research lab, we found a way to do this. I remembered a trick used in pruning the computation of unweighted Jaccard values by Theobald et al. [27] in their Stanford paper on news story deduplication, and realized that it was applicable to this problem:

In that SpotSigs paper [27], Theobald noticed that two documents of significantly different length could not have high Jaccard similarity. In particular, they noticed that

$$\frac{\|A \cap B\|}{\|A \cup B\|}$$

was at most

$$\frac{\|A\|}{\|B\|},$$

because this could only be increasing the numerator and decreasing the denominator.

Extending this idea to

$$\frac{\sum_{f \in A \cup B} \min(n_f^A, n_f^B)}{\sum_{f \in A \cup B} \max(n_f^A, n_f^B)},$$

we note that this is at most

$$\frac{\sum_{f \in A} n_f^A}{\sum_{f \in B} n_f^B}$$

for similar reasons: for positive numbers, this latter fraction again could only increase the numerator and decrease the denominator, both of which increase the ratio.

The numerator and denominator are simply the 1-norms of n^A and n^B, instead of the norms of the pointwise minimum and maximum of these values.

Randomized rounding [23] is the technique of replacing a real number r with fractional part f by $\lceil r \rceil$ with probability f and by $\lfloor r \rfloor$ with probability $1 - f$. This is 1-norm preserving in expectation, but changes the expected value of the maximum of two distributions slightly, leading to a small bias in estimation, due to inexact values for the expectation of the maximum of two approximated values..

Moreover, if we replace the weights n_f^A and n_f^B by versions scaled by k, this is Jaccard preserving:

$$\frac{\sum_{f \in A \cup B} \min(n_f^A, n_f^B)}{\sum_{f \in A \cup B} \max(n_f^A, n_f^B)} = \frac{\sum_{f \in A \cup B} \min(k n_f^A, k n_f^B)}{\sum_{f \in A \cup B} \max(k n_f^A, k n_f^B)}$$

whenever either (and thus both) of these fractions is defined; testing the similarity of two empty documents raises few issues.

Scaling is *not* norm-preserving in expectation: the 1-norm of a weighting multiplied by k is k times the 1-norm of the original weighting. After randomized rounding (which is, as stated, norm preserving in expectation), the 1-norm is unchanged in expectation (but is certain to be an integer, which we can view as a replication factor for each term in the weighting).

Weightings with 1-norms differing by more than a multiple of two cannot have Jaccard similarity exceeding one-half. Weightings with 1-norms differing by less than a factor of two are guaranteed to have integer scalings by identical or adjacent powers of two so that the 1-norms of both scalings fall into the range [4096, 16384]. Accordingly, the 1-norms of the randomized rounding of similarly normed weightings can be certain to have at least one common scaling by an integer power of two with both norms falling into the range [4096, 16384].

Given such a scaling, when we apply randomized rounding to replace each weight by an integer between 0 and 16383, we can view an input sequence as a set of a few thousand individual entries with unit weight, corresponding to $t_{i,j}$, where t_i is the ith input term from the initial distribution, and $0 \leq j < r_i$, where r_i is the rounded value of that scaled value of $n_{t_i}^A$.

Due to this scaling, if we are trying to produce 256 samples by generating a byte of randomness to choose a bin, the expected total weight after scaling and randomized rounding is at least 4096. The expected weight per bin is therefore at least $4096/256 = 16$. If the lead bytes are chosen randomly, we expect all 4096 units to miss some bin with probability at most $\left(\frac{255}{256}\right)^{4096} \approx e^{-\frac{4096}{256}} = e^{-16} \approx 1\mathrm{E} - 7$. Even accounting for the 256 different bins we expect that we will see a completely empty bin fewer than twice in a thousand documents. If the corpus size is very large, and the 1-norms barely exceed a power of two, we may want to reduce this probability, by scaling up by an extra factor of two or four. In any case, in most documents, the number of empty bins will rarely exceed 1, and we can remember which individual bin is empty and exclude it from comparisons; remembering two or three empty bins should suffice for nearly every document even in extremely large corpora.

A more careful examination of the resulting bias and standard deviation appears in a paper [9] Bernhard, Kunal, and I wrote while still at Microsoft.

Recent preprints by Li suggest that replicating selected min-hashes to empty bins by picking the same value as the preceding (in circular order) non-empty bin doesn't change the results too dramatically. An even-newer preprint extends Li's unweighted kernel methods to the weighted case.

Afterword

Thanks for persisting with this mixed bag of algorithms, mathematical curiosities, and algorithms engineering. I mean this in the best spirit of the HAKMEM collection of similar oddities from the MIT AI lab forty years ago. I hope that you have learned a few new algorithmic tricks for your arsenal. If you have, I hope you find interesting areas in which to apply them, although I have to give one final word of warning: many pieces of the algorithms examined herein are covered by a variety of U.S. and international patents. As such, experimental and investigational uses can be made without worrying about licensing. If you intend to use these techniques in a product, consult your attorney first.

Best wishes.

Bibliography

[1] Michael Beeler, R. William Gosper, and Richard Schroeppel (1972) HAKMEM, Artificial Intelligence Memo No. 239, February, Massachusetts Institute of Technology. http://www.inwap.com/pdp10/hbaker/hakmem/hakmem.html

[2] Andrei Z. Broder, Steven C. Glassman, Mark S. Manasse, and Geoffrey Zweig (1997) Syntactic Clustering of the Web, *J. Computer Networks*, volume 29, number 8–13, pp. 1157–1166. http://dx.doi.org/10.1016/S0169-7552(97)00031-7 DOI: 10.1016/S0169-7552(97)00031-7 70

[3] Ondre Chum, James Phibin, and Andrew Zisserman (2008) Near Duplicate Image Detection: min-Hash and tf-idf Weighting, in *British Machine Vision Conference*, Leeds, England. http://www.bmva.org/bmvc/2008/papers/119.pdf

[4] Edith Cohen and Haim Kaplan (2012) What you can do with Coordinated Samples, *J. CoRR*, volume abs/1206.5637. http://arxiv.org/abs/1206.5637

[5] Søren Dahlgaard and Mikkel Thorup (2014) Approximately Minwise Independence with Twisted Tabulation, in *14th Scandinavian Symposium and Workshops*, Copenhagen, Denmark, pp. 134–145. http://dblp.uni-trier.de/rec/bib/conf/swat/DahlgaardT14 xv

[6] Philippe Flajolet and G. Nigel Martin (1985) Probabilistic Counting Algorithms for Data Base Applications. in *J. Comput. Syst. Sci.*, volume 31, pp. 182–209. 70

[7] Aristides Gionis, Piotr Indyk, and Rajeev Motwani (1999) Similarity Search in High Dimensions via Hashing, in *VLDB*, Edinburgh, Scotland, pp. 518–529.

[8] Srinivas Gollapudi and Rina Panigrahy (2006) Exploiting asymmetry in hierarchical topic extraction, in *CIKM*, Sydney, Australia, pp. 475-482. DOI: 10.1145/1183614.1183683

[9] Bernhard Haeupler, Mark Manasse, and Kunal Talwar Consistent Weighted Sampling Made Fast, Small, and Easy in arXiv:1410.4266. http://arxiv.org/abs/1410.4266 72

[10] Nevin Heintze (1996) Scalable Document Fingerprinting, in *Proc. USENIX Workshop on Electronic Commerce*, Oakland, California, pp. 191-200.

[11] Piotr Indyk and Rajeev Motwani (1998) Approximate Nearest Neighbors: Towards Removing the Curse of Dimensionality, *STOC*, Dallas, Texas, pp. 604–613. http://doi.acm.org/10.1145/276698.276876 DOI: 10.1145/276698.276876

[12]   Piotr Indyk, Rajeev Motwani, Prabhakar Raghavan, and Santosh Vempala (1997) Locality-Preserving Hashing in Multidimensional Spaces, *STOC*, El Paso, Texas, pp. 618–625. `http://doi.acm.org/10.1145/258533.258656` DOI: 10.1145/258533.258656

[13]   Sergey Ioffe (2010) Improved Consistent Sampling, Weighted Minhash and L1 Sketching, in *ICDM*, Sydney, Australia, pp. 246–255. `http://doi.ieeecomputersociety.org/10.1109/ICDM.2010.80` DOI: 10.1109/ICDM.2010.80

[14]   Charles E. Leiserson, Harald Prokop, and Keith H. Randall (1998) Using de Bruijn Sequences to Index a 1 in a Computer Word, unpublished manuscript, but available as download, June, Massachusetts Institute of Technology. `http://supertech.csail.mit.edu/papers/debruijn.pdf`

[15]   Ping Li and Christian König (2010) b-Bit Minwise Hashing, in *WWW*. Raleigh, North Carolina, pp. 671–680.

[16]   Ping Li, Art B. Owen, and Cun-Hui Zhang (2012) One Permutation Hashing, in *NIPS* 26. Lake Tahoe, Nevada, pp. 3122–3130. 70

[17]   Mark Manasse, Frank McSherry, and Kunal Talwar (2010) Consistent Weighted Sampling, Tech. Report, number MSR-TR-2010-73, June, Microsoft Research. `http://research.microsoft.com/apps/pubs/default.aspx?id=132309`

[18]   Udi Manber (1994) Finding similar files in a large file system, in *USENIX Winter*, San Francisco, California, pp. 1–10.

[19]   Ralph C. Merkle (1989) A certified digital signature in *Proc. Advances in Cryptology*, pp. 218-238.

[20]   Rasmus Pagh and Flemming Friche Rodler (2004), Cuckoo hashing, *J. Algorithms*, Volume 51, Issue 2, May, pp. 122-144.

[21]   Mihai Pătrașcu and Mikkel Thorup (2011) The Power of Simple Tabulation Hashing, in *STOC*, San Jose, California, pp. 1–10. `http://arxiv.org/abs/1011.5200`

[22]   M. O. Rabin (1981) Fingerprinting by Random Polynomials, Tech. Report, number TR-15-81, Center for Research in Computing Technology, Harvard University.

[23]   Prabhakar Raghavan and Clark D. Tompson (1987), Randomized rounding: A technique for provably good algorithms and algorithmic proofs, Combinatorica 7(4), pp. 364-374. Raghavan

[24]   Saul Schleimer, Daniel Shawcross Wilkerson, and Alexander Aiken (2003) Winnowing: Local Algorithms for Document Fingerprinting, *SIGMOD Conference*, San Diego, California, pp. 76–85. `http://doi.acm.org/10.1145/872757.872770` DOI: 10.1145/872757.872770

[25] David B. Shmoys, Eva Tardos, and Karen Aardal (1998), Approximation algorithms for facility location problems (Extended Abstract), *STOC*, Dallas, Texas, pp. 256-274. `http://www.cs.cornell.edu/home/eva/facility.ps`

[26] Dan Teodosiu, Nikolaj Bjørner, Joe Porkka, Mark Manasse, and Yuri Gurevich (2006), Optimizing File Replication over Limited-Bandwidth Networks using Remote Differential Compression, Tech Report, number MSR-TR-2006-157, November, Microsoft Research. `http://research.microsoft.com/apps/pubs/default.aspx?id=64692`

[27] Martin Theobald, Jonathan Siddharth, and Andreas Paepcke (2008) SpotSigs: Robust and Efficient Near Duplicate Detection in Large Web Collections, in *SIGIR*, Seattle, Washington, pp. 563-570. 71

Author's Biography

MARK MANASSE

Mark Manasse was a Principal Researcher at Microsoft Research, which he joined in 2001, while writing the first edition of this book, and where he performed the research presented in the additional chapters that comprise the additional work presented in this second edition.

From 1985 until he joined Microsoft, Mark was a researcher at Compaq's Systems Research Center in Palo Alto, California (previously Digital Equipment Corporation, subsequently Hewlett-Packard and now extinct).

Mark worked at Microsoft until late 2014. He is now a Principal Architect (working on infrastructure security) at Salesforce®, which he thanks for their support while writing the final chapter of this second edition.

Mark Manasse works in a variety of theory-related areas of distributed computer systems research. He was the inventor of MilliCent; as such, Wired Magazine dubbed him "the guru of micropayments," and he was co-chair of the microcommerce working group for the World Wide Web Consortium. Mark has worked on Web search technologies; with Andrei Broder, Steve Glassman, and Geoff Zweig, his work on syntactic similarity was awarded best paper at the Sixth International World Wide Web Conference. Mark was a member the design committee for the Inter-Client Communications Manual for the X Window System. Mark's work on on-line algorithms helped to establish this field, and remain among his most often cited papers. Mark organized, ran, and developed much of the code for some of the earliest uses of the Internet in distributed computations when he and Arjen Lenstra factored many large integers, the most noteworthy being the first factorization of a "hard" 100-digit number, and the factorization of the ninth Fermat number; for several years thereafter, Mark's license plate read "IDIDF9," leaving most other drivers puzzled.

Mark holds U.S. patents in three of the previously mentioned areas. His doctorate was earned at the University of Wisconsin in Mathematical Logic in 1982, and he spent the following three years at Bell Labs and the University of Chicago.

Mark's projects after joining Microsoft included Koh-i-Noor, PageTurner, Dryad, a minor role in Penny Black, and work in various unnamed projects. Additionally, Mark worked on aspects of deduplication with product groups in MSN Search (now Bing) and with the Windows Server group on aspects of file systems and storage, starting with Windows Server 2003, and continuing through Windows 8.

In 1994, Newsweek described Severe Tire Damage (the band Mark helped found and for which he played bass) as "lesser-known" than the Rolling Stones, following STD's unauthorized appearance as the opening act in a multicast performance headlined by the Stones. The band is content with that.

Photo credit: Mihai Budiu.

Printed in the United States
by Baker & Taylor Publisher Services